NOT JUST A ✓ IN A B☐X

ANDREW FOY

Copyright © 2013 Andrew Foy. All rights reserved.
This edition published in 2013 by Foy Certification Ltd.

Website: www.foycertification .com
Twitter: www.twitter.com/andrewrfoy
Facebook: www.facebook.com/foycertification

Typeset in Lato Regular and Lato Bold by Karen Arnott, Graphic Designer,
14a High Street, West Wratting, Cambridge. CB21 5LU.

Illustrations © Richard Bowring (www.richardbowring.co.uk)
Cover design and book layout © Karen Arnott (www.karenarnott.co.uk)

ISBN 978-0-9576562-0-8

A Cataloguing-in-Publication record is available for this book from the British Library.

No part of this publication may be reproduced or transmitted in any form or by any means, or stored in any retrieval system of any nature without prior written permission, except for permitted fair dealing under the Copyright, Designs and Patents Act 1988, or in accordance with the terms issued by the Copyright Licensing Agency in respect of photocopying and/or reprographic reproduction. Application for permission for other use of copyright material including permissions to reproduce extracts in other published works shall be made to the publishers. Full acknowledgement of author, publisher and source must be given.

Material is contained in this publication for which publishing permission has been sought and for which copyright is acknowledged. Permission to reproduce such material cannot be granted by the publishers and application must be made to the copyright holder.

For Claire, Maddy, Annabelle and Fraser

My Why?

Acknowledgements

Thanks to my Customers...

Jim, Kelly, Mike L, Pete H, Rik, Tim C, Alexandra, Jeff, Ray, Lorraine, Alan, Julian, Dom, Rob M, Dave B, Howard, Alison, Phil O, Debbie O, Bernadette, Ken, Kevin, Richard, Tim H, Patrick, Debbie R, Sam, Paul B, Gillian, Sean, Stephen, Mike F, Manny, Sue, Dave R, Rob S, Adam, Samantha, Lee O, Malcolm, Gary, Andy, Jayne S, Matt B, Lee M, Paul D, Phil W, Clive, Kellie, Pete S, Nick, Paul L, Simon, Emma, Rachel, Steve, Mike D, Robert, Jonathan, Phil M, Matt, Jayne N, Matt F, Lee M, Ian, Mike P, Phyllis and Tom

...and my Reviewers...

David, Steve, Joe, Jonathan, Keith, Barry, Richard, Paul, Patrick, Mike, Phyllis, Adrian and of course...The Big Fella

Reviews

"Easy to follow which is great, would be useful to Board Directors who are looking at the details and benefits of ISO Certification before making a decision to commit"
Joe Cilia, Technical Manager, Association of Interior Specialists (AIS)

"Clever, witty, friendly and concise. This is an easy to follow and interesting approach, guaranteed to catch your attention and turn you into an instant ISO addict with a very prosperous future!"
Phyllis Boardman, CEO, Green Deal Consortia

"Enough to convince every subcontractor that ISO Certification is not only achievable but highly desirable"
Jonathan Green, Managing Director, ISOlite Certification Ltd (UKAS Accredited Certification Body)

"Does a great job of explaining, in simple terms, the benefits of fitting ISOs to the reader's business"
David Pickering, Director, David Pickering Strategy Limited

"Anyone thinking of embarking on an ISO journey should read this book first. Anyone struggling with implementation should get their teams to read this book. Simple, clear and logical. Brilliant"
Paul Little, Managing Director, Coen Ltd

"Although it is a business book, and so could be in danger of being "dry", it's not. All of this invaluable information flows into you as it's an easy read, well-pitched, plain English and devoid of unnecessary jargon."
Richard Catt, CEO, Contract Flooring Association

"Achieves its objective. Makes a big complex subject simple without being simplistic"
Steve Halcrow, Director of the FPDC

Contents

	About The Author	i
1.	Introduction	1
2.	Using This Book	7
3.	So What's It All About?	11
	Summary	15
4.	We Need To Talk About Quality Management Principles	17
	Summary	25
5.	Quality Management	27
	Summary	41
6.	Environmental Management	43
	Summary	52
7.	Occupational Health & Safety Management	53
	Summary	61
8.	PAS2030	63
	Summary	68
9.	Get Integrated	69
	Summary	73
10.	Show Me The Benefits	75
	Summary	83
11.	Geek Mythology	85
	Summary	105
12.	What Not To Do	107
	Summary	116
13.	The Only Way Is UKAS	117
	Summary	122
14.	The 8 Step Methodology	123
	Summary	145
15.	It's The Improvement, STUPID!	147
	Summary	161
	Testimonials	163
	What To Do Next	167

About The Author

Andrew Foy worked for and alongside specialist subcontractors for over twenty years.

He is a Member of the Chartered Institute of Building (MCIOB) and a qualified Lead Auditor for ISO 9001, ISO 14001 and OHSAS 18001.

His time is spent not on auditing however. As the owner of Foy Certification he is on a mission to help as many specialist subcontractors as possible to gain ISO and other Certifications that will open up new markets, assure customers, manage risks and improve specialists' businesses.

Introduction

This book is written **by** a specialist construction subcontractor (OK, ex-subcontractor) **for** specialist construction subcontractors. Why, because I believe that in the brutal world of construction subcontracting, specialists, of any size and any sector, can benefit enormously from Quality Management and Quality Management Principles and indeed from securing ISO Certification (i.e. being independently assessed) to the International Standards that our industry increasingly demands, namely ISO 9001 (Quality Management), ISO 14001 (Environmental Management) and OHSAS 18001 (Health & Safety Management). Certification to these Standards can cut-through the current bane of subcontractor's lives — filling in pre-qualification questionnaires (PQQ's). Not just filling them in either, ISO Certification greatly increases your chances of getting on that next tender list from a particular customer who doesn't currently work with your business. Most of the questions I see on PQQ's ask for evidence of precisely the sort of business activities and practices that automatically come through developing a Quality Management System (QMS) certified to ISO 9001 or preferably an Integrated Management System (IMS) certified to ISO 9001/ISO 14001/OHSAS 18001. Even if users of PQQ's

Chapter 1 — Introduction

do not specifically ask that you be certified, they then go on to demand that you conduct your operations doing largely what the Standards ask you to do anyway! Certification normally allows you to sail through most of the PQQ's and let's face it, they are not going to go away. Ensuring the quality of the supply chain is becoming increasingly important for employers of specialist suppliers and subcontractors and there seems to be no choice other than for these businesses to get professional about assuring their potential customers. ISO Certification however is certainly **Not Just a Tick in a Box** on a PQQ.

I spent over twenty years as a specialist subcontractor. I learnt by performing many different roles within rapidly expanding companies, culminating in becoming a Chartered Member of the Institute of Building (MCIOB) in 1997. I have worked with all levels of customer and helped to build and lead businesses through good times and bad. I am also a qualified Lead Auditor for all three Standards (ISO 9001 (Quality Management), ISO 14001 (Environmental Management) and OHSAS 18001 (Health & Safety Management)) but I am not interested in auditing. I undertook the auditor qualifications in order to look the auditors in the eye of behalf of my customers — businesses like yours.

Having successfully implemented these Standards into construction sub-contracting businesses I have become a passionate believer in their power to control, improve and grow a specialist construction business. But often, implementation is bureaucratic, irrelevant and inappropriate to the business needs, and offers nothing for the future (we will look at this in detail in chapter 12). That is the polar extreme to my approach and it gives me great pleasure to say that the combination of practical experience of having implemented the Standards and the theoretical knowledge from being a qualified Lead Auditor is proving invaluable to contributing to my mission of helping other subcontractors' enjoy the benefits and opportunities of successful ISO Certification.

Chapter 1 – Introduction

In the modern construction industry there is no project that is divorced from Quality, Health & Safety and Environmental issues. The quality angle speaks for itself as today's customers won't expect anything less than a quality installation delivered in a demonstrably quality manner throughout. The real advances the industry has made over the last twenty years in terms of Health & Safety performance, equally mean that demonstrable Health & Safety Management is also essential for any serious contractor. The enormous ongoing societal change to a culture of recycling and other green considerations impacts the construction industry arguably more than any other; and the UK construction industry in the eyes of many is now leading the way. From building owners to main contractors down to construction specialists, acquiring and displaying your green credentials is an essential prerequisite of tender and project success. All this of course is against a background of increasingly stringent Health & Safety and Environmental legislation.

So the smallest of subcontractors has to think of more than his technical expertise in his chosen field. He has to assure his customers of a quality delivery, and also show that he is a safe pair of hands in Health & Safety and Environmental terms when he becomes part of the whole supply chain.

The requirements of ISO 9001 have immediate application and relevance to construction specialists. ISO 14001 and OHSAS 18001 could have been written for the industry; especially given the enormous focus on Health & Safety performance over the last twenty years which of course is ongoing and is unlikely to become less pressured; and the more recent, but equally demanding requirement, for demonstrable management of Environmental performance.

Many construction specialist companies are founded by ex-craftsmen, or technical men and women whose skills in providing their product or service in their chosen field are undoubted; and they just want to get on with providing that product or service. But as we saw above this is not enough in the modern

Chapter 1 — Introduction

industry. Clients take technical expertise for granted, that is the minimum requirement to be even considered for a project. Customers want to be assured by a demonstration of your ability, as a businessman as well as a craftsman, to deliver quality consistently i.e. your Quality Management System.

The ISO Standards, the ones relevant to us as construction specialists — ISO 9001, ISO 14001 and OHSAS 18001 — offer the specialist a ready-made framework for Quality, Health & Safety and Environmental Management. The gifted craftsman need look no further in order to develop a comprehensive Management System for his company to assure his customers and manage his (and therefore, as his employer) his customer's risks. Furthermore, he can rest assured that industry experts have contributed to the formulation of the Standards and taken his needs into account.

Chapter 1 — Introduction

Every good contractor deserves recognition. I take good contractors through a process of fitting the ISO Standards to their business not expecting their business to fit to ISO. Invariably, it is a simpler and more rewarding experience, offering immediate benefits to their businesses, than most subcontractors imagine at the outset. Together, we build a lean and practical Integrated Management System from the bottom up: starting with what the business needs, enshrining best practice appropriate to that business and leading to independent Certification to the three main Standards, and indeed other Standards and specifications that are springing up around the Green Deal such as PAS2030 (see chapter 8). Being **Not Just a Tick in a Box**, Certification is about customer assurance, risk management, opening up new markets and customers of course, but, most importantly, instilling business improvement processes that build long-term value. Certification gives the organisation the benefit of an independent and objectively evaluated assessment of your Quality Management System. Better still, it is a very public declaration of your commitment to Quality that is universally understood and accepted.

Chapter 1 — Introduction

Fit ISO to your business; don't fit your business to ISO

Using This Book

I have made this book as user friendly as possible.

Wherever I can sensibly avoid it I do not use ISO jargon although I must include a few definitions below.

I do use the term "ISO" for example, "ISO expects you to ...." or "If you decide to go for ISO ..." as meaning the whole process of developing a Management System and seeking Certification.

Although the book works as a continuous narrative, each chapter stands alone as well, so it can be picked up at will. This inevitably means there will be an element of repetition, but in a way that reinforces the points being made. The chapter summaries assist this idea of diving in and out.

I use the term Quality Management System (QMS) mostly, although this should be read as being interchangeable with Integrated Management System (IMS) in most situations. For reasons I will explain, I urge any business starting

Chapter 2 — Using This Book

from scratch in ISO terms to develop an Integrated Management System from the start.

I use 9001 to mean ISO 9001:2008; 14001 to mean ISO 14001:2004 and 18001 to mean OHSAS 18001:2007 i.e. meaning the current version of the relevant Standards at the time of going to press.

I have included information on PAS2030, the Certification required by installers of energy efficiency measures under the Green Deal. Not only will the Green Deal become a major feature of the industry over the coming years (albeit with some teething problems to overcome) it is also the case that the requirements of PAS2030 are full of ISO Principles and indeed fit well within an Integrated Management System.

There is a chapter on the role of Auditors and the United Kingdom Accreditation Service (UKAS) but I also refer to those processes and bodies beforehand so a few definitions are appropriate:

The United Kingdom Accreditation Service "accredits" what are called Certification Bodies (Auditors) who will then "certify" businesses like yours. So although many people refer to ISO accreditation in a generic sense, the correct term is "Certification" for individual businesses (the term "accreditation" being reserved for Certification Bodies). You may also come across the term "registration", some commentators will talk about "your ISO registration" meaning your successful Certification to one or more of the ISO Standards.

When a business seeks registration for the first time it must undergo a two-stage audit. Stage 1 is a document review, which is a desk based audit by an Auditor of your Quality Management System and paperwork. This is to check the compliance of your manual and associated paperwork against the requirements of the Standards.

Chapter 2 — Using This Book

Stage 2 is a "live test" of the system you have created where an Auditor will check that you do what you say do i.e. that your operations conform to your stated business activities.

Unless explicitly stated otherwise, any quotations are only from the ISO website and/or the actual ISO Standards themselves.

So What's It All About?

If we are going to read about the power of ISO Standards to help control, develop and grow a specialist construction business then we have to spend a little time on some basics.

So what's it all about? The ISO's website (www.iso.org) tells us, "ISO (International Organization for Standardization) is the world's largest developer of International Standards which give state of the art specifications for products, services and good practice, covering almost all aspects of technology and business and helping to make industry more efficient and effective".

Sounds good doesn't it?

"ISO Standards make a positive contribution to the world we live in. They ensure vital features such as quality, ecology, safety, economy, reliability, compatibility, interoperability, efficiency and effectiveness. They facilitate trade, spread knowledge, and share technological advances and good management practices".

Chapter 3 — So What's It All About?

Well what a good start! If we are involved in any industry, or activity, of any kind we would surely want to be "more efficient and effective". In the recently brutal world of low-margin construction, that is not an aspiration it is a prerequisite for survival.

Back to the ISO's website; "We are a network of national Standards bodies. These national Standards bodies make up the ISO membership and they represent ISO in their country". In the UK the application of ISO Rules and Standards is under the control of UKAS, the United Kingdom Accreditation Service (www.ukas.com). We will look at the role of UKAS later on but suffice to say that UKAS, here in the UK, administers the application of International Standards.

More background. Everyone talks of ISO rather than IOS, which would be the acronym for the 'International Organization for Standardization'. Why? Because 'International Organization for Standardization' would have different acronyms in different languages (IOS in English, OIN in French for Organisation internationale de normalisation). So the founders decided to give it the short form ISO. ISO is derived from the Greek isos, meaning equal. Whatever the country, whatever the language, the short form is always ISO.

What is a Standard?

"A Standard is a document that provides requirements, specifications, guidelines or characteristics that can be used consistently to ensure that materials, products, processes and services are fit for their purpose". It's getting better don't you think? I'm sure you would agree that our customers want to know that our products, processes and services are fit for purpose. To have our offerings therefore assessed against a universally acknowledged appropriate "Standard" is therefore one way of our customers being assured that we are a safe pair of hands to engage and do business with.

Chapter 3 — So What's It All About?

As we are concerned primarily with the needs of specialist subcontractors and suppliers, and as the most relevant Standards for those businesses are ISO 9001 (Quality Management), ISO 14001 (Environmental Management) and OHSAS 18001 (Health & Safety Management), plus PAS2030 for installations under the Green Deal and which is also administered by UKAS, we will look in detail at the requirements and benefits of all those Standards in forthcoming chapters.

In purely general terms, and we are back to our friendly website here, "ISO International Standards ensure that products and services are safe, reliable and of good quality". You can't argue with that can you? "For business, they are strategic tools that reduce costs by minimizing waste and errors and increasing productivity". Can't really argue with that either! "They help companies to access new markets". Anybody want to access new markets?

A bit more background and then we'll move on. "Standards are developed by the people that need them, through a consensus process. Experts from all over the world develop the Standards that are required by their sector. This means they reflect a wealth of international experience and knowledge". You can rest assured that the best brains in the country have been involved in the development of our appropriate Standards. Standards that are needed by society, by business sectors and indeed by the government will be identified and will be developed with relevant sector partners. Which means that expertise will be brought in by those who understand the needs for the Standards and the desired ramifications of the effort in implementing them and putting them to use. It is this approach that makes ISO Standards broadly respected and implemented domestically and internationally, and by both private and public sectors.

Dig in a bit longer as there are other things you can't argue with. The Quality Management Standard 9001 and other Standards that have a Quality Management System as fundamental to their effective application are based on Eight Quality Management Principles which can be used as a guide for

Chapter 3 — So What's It All About?

improving business performance. These Principles are derived from the collective experience of international experts so we'd expect them to stand up to scrutiny.

Sounds too good to be true doesn't it? Applying ISO Standards seems to be promising us more efficiency, more effectiveness, making us fit for purpose, safer and more reliable, minimising waste and errors and increasing productivity. Moreover these Standards claim to be based on principles that we can use as a guide for improving overall business performance. Can we afford not to take all this very seriously? Can main contractors and Local Authorities and others who use our services afford not to insist that we do?

We need to talk about these Quality Management Principles so we'll do that in the next chapter.

Summary

So what's it all about...

- Efficiency
- Effectiveness
- Safety
- Reliability
- Increasing productivity
- Assuring customers
- Accessing new markets
- Managing risks
- Improving our business...
- (among other things!)

4

We Need To Talk About Quality Management Principles

Chapter 4 — We Need To Talk About Quality Management Principles

The Eight Quality Management Principles that form the basis of the Quality Management Standards are:

1. Customer Focus

2. Leadership

3. Involvement of People

4. Process Approach

5. System Approach to Management

6. Continual Improvement

7. Factual Approach to Decision Making

8. Mutually Beneficial Supplier Relationships.

Who wants to start the arguing? Or should we explore each Principle a little bit more to see if we can hang our hat on anything?

According to ISO, what is the thinking behind each Principle when formulating the Standards? We have to know to see if it can help our specialist construction businesses.

1. Customer focus

So what we do we mean by Customer Focus? I think we can safely say that businesses depend on their customers, not that you'd notice in some organisations. Shouldn't we understand, completely and comprehensively, our customer's current and future needs? I do mean really understand! Can we say we fully know our customer's requirements and how to meet them? Shouldn't we make sure that we do? Doesn't the success — indeed the very survival of our businesses — depend on striving to meet and exceed our customer's expectations? Pretty difficult to do so without a genuine "customer focus". We can expect therefore that 9001, in particular, will offer us some practical assistance in engendering a Customer Focus.

What might all this lovely Customer Focus lead to? Well would you accept that a perceptive grasp of what our customers want not only increases our chances of meeting and exceeding expectations but might also give us better ability to respond to market opportunities in a fast and flexible way? Furthermore, wouldn't that lead to increased revenue and market share?

That understanding would surely make us more effective and efficient in the use of our resources in enhancing customer satisfaction. Wouldn't customer satisfaction lead to customer loyalty and from there onto repeat business?

2. Leadership

I wonder how much has been written on the subject of Leadership. It's not my place to add to that, but to briefly look at Leadership as a Quality Management Principle and in the context of specialist contractors attempting to apply the Requirements of the International Standards. If nothing else the MD or Owner establishes the direction of the organisation. Whether he or she realises it or not, he should also be ensuring unity of purpose, that everyone knows what they are doing and why. The leader creates the organisation's internal environment, its culture — sometimes by default! Surely we want an internal environment in which people can become fully involved in achieving the business's objectives. That will bring understanding and motivation towards the business's goals. We want alignment not miscommunication and that comes from Leadership.

Chapter 4 — We Need To Talk About Quality Management Principles

The need for strong Leadership and its role in the International Standards will become apparent throughout the rest of this book. How are you leading your business? Does everyone know what is expected and how they contribute? Do they know where your business is going?

3. Involvement of people

Aren't people always involved? Well yes, but are they engaged? "People are our greatest asset" is the platitude often wheeled out, but it never ceases to amaze me how often it is not appreciated. Some organisations are able to acknowledge that, yes of course, people at all levels are the essence of an organisation but then fail to realise that their full involvement and engagement enables their abilities — if appreciated — to be used for the organisation's benefit. The Standards talk endlessly about involving your people; making them aware of what you are trying to do; communicating effectively with them; wrapping processes around their roles and responsibilities; encouraging their contribution to your best practice; training them and enhancing their competence. Are you happy with how "involved" your people are?

4. Process approach

What on earth do we mean by a Process Approach? This is the sort of language that turns some people off. Very simply a "process" can be described as taking some inputs, doing something to them and churning out some outputs. I agree that, for some, "inputs" and "outputs" are not the easiest of words but I think we can all understand what that means, and isn't that we do in our businesses? We take tender documents, bills of quantity and specifications for example, apply our knowledge, experience and estimating processes, and create the output of a compliant tender document. Processes on sites - in terms of inputs and outputs - are even more obvious. The Standards are based on the simple process philosophy of Plan-Do-Check & Act.

Chapter 4 — We Need To Talk About Quality Management Principles

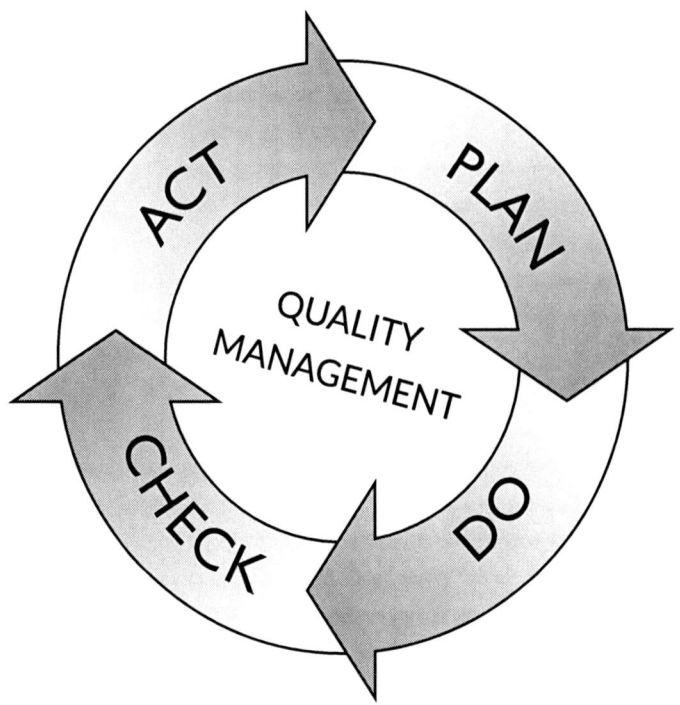

Basic ISO Philosophy of Plan-Do-Check & Act

When this process is applied to a business as a whole think of the "Plan" as preparing your business to enter the market, the "Do" as clearly providing your product or service and the "Check and Act" as monitoring your performance and seeking to improve on it based on your observations. The Standards declare that, "When activities are managed as a process desired results are achieved more efficiently, resources are used more effectively, results are more consistent and predictable, and improvement opportunities can be spotted and concentrated on more easily". Really? We will see if and how the Standards help us to achieve this.

Chapter 4 — We Need To Talk About Quality Management Principles

5. A System approach to management

More jargon I'm afraid, who's getting turned off? A System Approach to Management means identifying, understanding and managing processes that link and follow on from each other - for example estimating and tendering, planning, installation, commercial management, training - as a system contributes to the organisation's effectiveness and efficiency in achieving its objectives. We all want to avoid overlap and underlap and have our processes flow smoothly through the best sequence we can come up with.

6. Continual improvement

I don't think anyone can argue with the concept of Continual Improvement. Surely Continual Improvement of the organisation's overall performance should be a permanent objective of any organisation. If you're not improving then what are you doing? Wiser heads than me say that you can't standstill in practice; you are either improving or deteriorating. If Continual Improvement is a bedrock Quality Management Principle underlying the Quality Management Standards then we should again expect some practical guidance from the Standards in knowing how to achieve it. I dwell on this later because if you had to boil down all the reasons why you should consider ISO Certification into just one then I would suggest that improving your business is that primary reason. Think about it; a business that is **continually improving**!

7. Factual approach to decision making

A Factual Approach to Decision Making? Don't we always make decisions based on the facts? I wonder. Are the facts always available? Effective decisions come from the analysis of data and information. An old MD of mine used to say to me as I put my monthly reports together that, "Quality information makes for quality decisions." What quality information do we need and where does it come from? Do we know what we need? Do we know how to get it? Have we really thought about it? This would suggest that the Standards look to providing the facts to aid decision-making. We'll need to bear that in mind when we read on, especially when we look at such things as the Requirements of the Standards and their effective implementation. Are you basing your decisions on appropriate "facts"?

8. Mutually beneficial supplier relationships

We all want Mutually Beneficial Supplier Relationships. But I've been treated appallingly by main contractors and also seen some colleagues not treat our own supply chain too respectfully. Any organisation and its suppliers are interdependent. A Mutually Beneficial Supplier Relationship enhances the ability of both to create value. We talked above (Principle no. 1) about the importance of Customer Focus and understanding what our customers want; do our suppliers and subcontractors know what **we** want? Do we tell them? Clearly? Do we know, really know, that we have the right suppliers? How do we choose our suppliers and subcontractors and how do we manage them? We cannot improve our customer service unless our customers give us feedback to work with; equally we owe it to our own suppliers and subcontractors (maybe that is just Labour Only Subcontractors for some organisations) to tell them what we want and constantly communicate with them about their performance.

So that was a quick general perspective on the Quality Management Principles underlying the ISO 9000 series in particular. Hopefully you can agree that the Principles, applied properly, can form a basis for performance improvement and organisational excellence. So having looked at the Quality Management Principles, we need to go on and see if the actual Standards 9001/14001/18001 embody them, and show us how they can guide us in improving the performance of our specialist construction businesses. The nature of the organisation and the specific challenges it faces will determine how to implement them, but I

Chapter 4 — We Need To Talk About Quality Management Principles

hope you can see that many organisations will find it beneficial to set up Quality Management Systems based on these Principles.

The authors of the International Standards have taken these Principles and incorporated them into suggested frameworks for managing our businesses. It is time to look at the requirements of each Standard in turn; both individual requirements and the requirements when viewed as a whole.

Summary

The Eight Quality Management Principles:

- Customer focus
- Leadership
- Involvement of people
- Process approach
- System approach to management
- Continual improvement
- Factual approach to decision making
- Mutually beneficial supplier relationships

Quality Management

The ISO 9000 family of Standards are arguably the most widely recognised. They address various elements of Quality Management, providing guidance and methods for organisations who consistently want to meet, and hopefully exceed, customer's requirements by ensuring that their products and services are always delivered to the highest standards. And of course that their service is continually improved, a fundamental Quality Management Principle as we have just seen.

There are many Standards in the ISO 9000 family but for our purposes we are interested in ISO 9001:2008 which sets out the requirements of a Quality Management System i.e. it is not specific to products or services, but applies to the business's processes that create and deliver them. This is the only member of the ISO 9001 family that organisations can seek independent Certification to.

This Standard can be used by any organisation, large or small, regardless of its business offering, and is based, on the Quality Management Principles we looked at in the previous chapter.

Chapter 5 — Quality Management

The effective application of ISO 9001:2008 will help to ensure that customers get consistent, good quality products and services. The business benefits to the construction specialist of doing so are obvious. ISO 9001 has also been steadily evolving as a method of assuring customers beforehand that "quality" will be achieved (as well as being a Standard designed to guide businesses to achieve that quality). Every customer may have a different set of criteria for a "quality" job but whichever way they define it your customers have to be happy with what you give them and increasingly these days want assurance that you have the business capability to deliver even before you are given the actual opportunity to do so! Is that not the point of Pre-Qualification Questionnaires (PQQ's)? So in this regard, ISO 9001 can be viewed as offering significant business benefits to your customer as well as to your organisation in applying it.

If you look beyond the jargon (which can be a little off-putting) and also beyond the clause references (which can be even more so), then in my view ISO 9001 is based on a logical process based format - remember our Quality Management Principle **Process Approach** - which can be easily used by any business.

The ISO 9000 family talks about the philosophy of Quality Management, about definitions and vocabulary, and also of course about the Eight Quality Management Principles discussed earlier. Although these Principles are not elements that are directly tested by an Auditor they are absolutely part of the fabric of ISO and are woven throughout the Standard. Even if an organisation did not want to go for independent Certification to 9001 it would need to pay heed to the Quality Management Principles to follow 9001 in spirit.

We will certainly look at the Requirements individually and in some detail, but to summarise ISO 9001 simply and succinctly, I would do so as follows:

- Commit — and that means not just talking-the-talk but obviously walking-the-talk i.e. to be the best your organisation can be in providing

Chapter 5 — Quality Management

and delivering its product or service, usually starting with a Quality Policy Statement

- Make sure you fully understand, without ambiguity, what your customer wants

- Ensure the means to deliver what your customer wants in terms of qualified personnel, appropriate infrastructure and work environment, and effective systems and processes

- Monitor your operations, seek input and feedback from your staff, operatives, suppliers, and most importantly your customers, on your delivery performance

- Commit to continually improve your performance through reviews of your effectiveness and by setting improvement objectives.

What do you think of that summary? Logical? Are there any elements of that summary that you wouldn't regard as worth doing? I would contend that you need to do all these things well in order to run your business successfully.

Obviously there are layers of detail for each of my summary points above and these will come out as we look at the individual requirements that all need to be addressed in order to become certified. So moving to the next level of detail, we should see 9001 as setting out the criteria for a Quality Management System i.e. what an effective Quality Management System needs to contain. This can be used by any organisation, of any size, and the essential point here is that it is done in a manner appropriate to **your** organisation. One of my clichés that my customers get sick of hearing is that my favourite word in the whole litany of ISO Standards and literature is "appropriate"! Nowhere does ISO imply that uniformity of documentation

Chapter 5 — Quality Management

or implementation is the intention; it is vital that what you do is appropriate to your business.

I could scream at the number of times I have seen a six-inch thick Quality Manual sat on a shelf gathering dust, being used by nobody in the three or four man business upon which it has been imposed. Don't get me started. In fact you don't need to as I have devoted a whole chapter to this later.

ISO 9001 is used by external parties, including Certification bodies (Auditors), to assess the organisation's ability to meet customer, statutory and regulatory requirements applicable to the product, and the organisation's own requirements as defined in the organisation's own Quality Management System. As mentioned earlier, Certification to ISO 9001 is seen as ensuring that customers get consistent, good quality products and services, which is why main contractors and Local Authorities use it as a pre-qualification tool. Organisations that secure independent UKAS (see chapter 13) accredited Certification to ISO 9001 can provide that customer assurance.

Any business serious about enhancing customer satisfaction can achieve ISO 9001 rapidly and cost-effectively. So let's get on with it. What specifically do we have to do?

Chapter 5 — Quality Management

My favourite word is "appropriate"

Chapter 5 — Quality Management

General requirements of quality management

First and foremost there needs to be a demonstrable Quality Management System (a clear way of running things) and the desire and capacity to continually improve its effectiveness.

This involves determining (**Plan** from our Plan-Do-Check & Act mentioned earlier as an example of Quality Management Principle **Process Approach**) and implementing (**Do**) processes for the Quality Management System, ensuring they are effective, providing resources and information for monitoring and analysing them (**Check**) and acting (and **Act**) to achieve planned results and continual improvement.

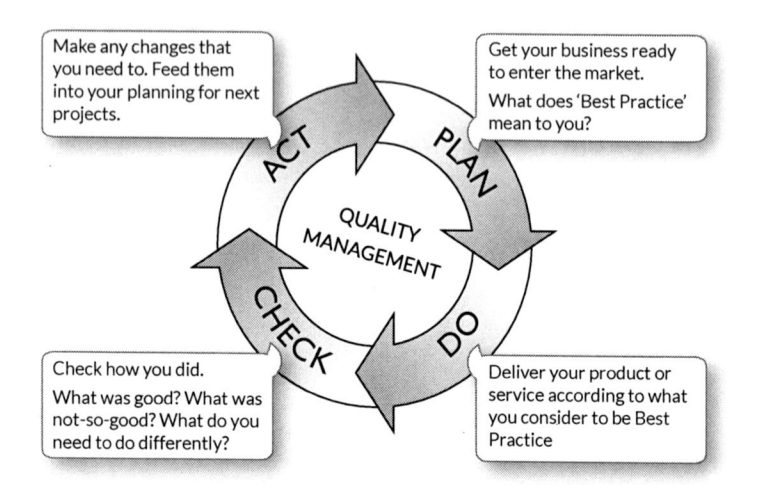

- Make any changes that you need to. Feed them into your planning for next projects.
- Get your business ready to enter the market. What does 'Best Practice' mean to you?
- Check how you did. What was good? What was not-so-good? What do you need to do differently?
- Deliver your product or service according to what you consider to be Best Practice

Plan-Do-Check & Act and Your Business

Just a quick note on sub-contracting, (or "outsourcing" as 9001 refers to it), be it labour only subcontractors - as is common throughout the construction industry - or even sub-contracting elements of your organisation's offering.

This is seen as legitimate as long as control is maintained by your organisation i.e. you do not take a customer's order and simply farm it off to ANOther and forget about it. I'm not suggesting you would do that but you can see the point about maintaining control. You would need to be clearly instructing your subcontractor, monitoring his performance and ensuring that **your** standards are maintained right up to Handover with **your** customer.

Specific requirements of quality management

Documentation requirements

Whilst it is not the intent of ISO 9001 to generate a complex documented system (one of the myths discussed later) there are of course **some** required documents, namely:

- a documented statement of a quality policy (see below and this is where Quality Management Principle **Customer Focus** can be declared)

- a Quality Manual of some sort, in any form or medium, but one that ensures effective planning, operation and control of its processes (Quality Management Principle **A System Approach to Management**)

- Quality Objectives (see below, Quality Management Principle **Continual Improvement**).

Control of Documents

Contrary to popular belief there are only Six Mandatory Documented Procedures in ISO 9001 and these could be written on two sides of A4.

The first of these is "control" of those documents that **are** generated; this centres mainly on ensuring the correct use of the right documents, and their being made available at the right time and for the right person. This is easily achieved with simple referencing and with simple rules as to how documents are generated and looked after.

The second Mandatory Procedure similarly relates to controlling records that your Quality Management System produces so that they are protected and readily identifiable and retrievable. Examples here would be O&M Manuals, Tool Box Talks, maybe Progress Reports. Some records will be demanded by ISO 9001 but most will be what **you** determine as being required to conduct your operations effectively.

Management responsibility and commitment

A fundamental ISO Principle (and of course a Quality Management Principle looked at earlier: **Leadership**) is that Top Management shall provide evidence of its commitment to the development and implementation of the Quality Management System and to continually improving (again) its effectiveness. This will involve communicating the importance of determining and meeting customer requirements with the aim of enhancing customer satisfaction (Customer Focus in action).

Other expectations of Top Management are as follows:

- Quality Policy — establishing, communicating and reviewing a Quality Policy that commits to customer focus, to complying with the Quality Management System requirements and continually improving performance. The Policy also provides a framework for establishing and reviewing Quality Objectives. This is your public declaration of your commitment to being a quality company and is the, usually one-page, statement that you will send out when prospective customers ask for your "Quality Policy" or "Quality Policy Statement"

Chapter 5 — Quality Management

- Quality Objectives — ensuring that Quality Objectives are established at relevant functions and levels within the organisation to ensure continual improvement. These are the improvements to your business that you want to make over the forthcoming period

- Quality Management System planning — ensuring that planning of your Quality Management is carried out so that your System best meets customer requirements, achieves the Quality Objectives you have identified and that the integrity of the Quality Management System is maintained (**A System Approach to Management**)

- Responsibility and authority — ensuring that responsibilities and authorities are defined and communicated within the organisation

- Management representative — appointing a member of the organisation's management as the "custodian" of the Quality Management System. This is certainly not identifying an individual who the whole process can be "dumped" upon; it is identifying someone who will seriously look after the system and who will be given the authority to do so

- Communication — ensuring that appropriate internal and external communication processes are established within the organisation

- Management Review — comprehensively reviewing the organisation's Quality Management System, at planned intervals, to ensure its continuing suitability, adequacy and effectiveness. Done correctly, Management Reviews represent a major and powerful improvement process (see chapter 13).

Resource management

Chapter 5 — Quality Management

The organisation needs to determine and provide the resources needed to implement, maintain and improve the Quality Management System and enhance customer satisfaction. ISO 9001 talks of maintaining the infrastructure and environment needed to achieve "conformity to product requirements", i.e. a decent and productive workplace with appropriate facilities needs to be provided.

Human resources and competence

Determining and demonstrating the competence of all personnel is another fundamental ISO Principle. But considering your human resources, your greatest asset, and how they feel involved (**Involvement of People!**) and engaged to effectively contribute to your business goes well beyond just competence.

Product/service realisation and provision

The organisation shall plan the processes needed for developing your product or service and providing it to customers. For example:

- determining, reviewing and meeting customer requirements

- planning and providing the resources required

- control of core business activities

- necessary support activities

- provision, maintenance and calibration of appropriate equipment

- customer communications

- inspection and test activities

- approval and handover

- record keeping.

Design and development

For those organisations that undertake design and development ISO 9001 is prescriptive about controlling and managing:

- the design and development stages, advising on inputs and outputs and the control of changes

- the review, verification and validation that are appropriate to each design and development stage, and

- the responsibilities and authorities for design and development.

Purchasing

Procurement is clearly fundamental to construction operations so it is not surprising that 9001 has a lot to say about the need for effective purchasing. The adequacy of specified purchase requirements needs to be established and demonstrated so that purchased items conform to specified purchase requirements. Alongside these requirements, is the need to evaluate and select suppliers and subcontractors based on their ability to supply what the organisation requires (**Mutually Beneficial Supplier Relationships**).

Monitoring and improvement

The organisation shall plan and implement the monitoring and improvement processes (**Factual Approach to Decision Making**) to demonstrate the performance of the Quality Management System, ensure conformity of the Quality Management System, and to continually improve the effectiveness of the Quality Management System. One of the measurements shall monitor information relating to customer perception as to whether the organisation has met customer requirements (customer satisfaction and feedback).

Internal audit

Checking that the System works is a vital part of ISO 9001:2008. An organisation must perform internal audits to check how its Quality Management System is working. An organisation may decide to invite an independent Certification Body to verify that it is in conformity to the Standard, but there is no requirement for this. Alternatively, it might invite its clients to audit the Quality Management System for themselves.

ISO 9001 expects the organisation to conduct internal audits at planned intervals to determine whether the Quality Management System a) conforms to the planned arrangements and to the requirements of 9001, and b) is effectively implemented and maintained. This represents a major improvement opportunity. A documented procedure, the third Mandatory Procedure, shall be established to define the responsibilities and requirements for planning and conducting audits, establishing records and reporting results.

The fourth Mandatory Documented Procedure relates to what is called "dealing with nonconformity" i.e. what arrangements the organisation has in place for when things go wrong. When non-conformances, or things that have gone wrong are discovered at, for example, internal audit then the fifth and sixth Mandatory Documented Procedures come into play which are corrective action (action to put things right) and preventive action (action to stop them going wrong in the first place) respectively.

Management review

At planned intervals (minimum yearly) you are expected to conduct a comprehensive review of your management system and its performance. This

Chapter 5 — Quality Management

is an opportunity to check your system's accuracy, suitability and effectiveness and to seek out recommendations for improvement.

Continual Improvement is arguably the most important ISO Principle of all and one of course that is impossible to argue with and leads to long-term business value. ISO 9001 expects an organisation to continually improve the effectiveness of the Quality Management System through its Policy, Quality Objectives, Monitoring, Internal Audits and Management Review.

A couple of technical points to consider:

Firstly, when you become certified to ISO 9001, you must make it clear which elements of your organisation are covered by your Certificate of Registration. For most small businesses the Certificate will cover your office activities and all your operations on your customers' sites. It is feasible however that you may have some ancillary services, or a satellite office that you do not wish to be covered by your registration as they do not form part of your core business. The Scope of Registration is the vehicle to making this clear, and it is very important that you do so.

Secondly, there are some circumstances under which certain ISO 9001 Requirements can be excluded, without precluding you from successful Certification. Exclusions can only come from section 7 which is all about physically providing and delivering your product and service. This section for example has rules about looking after a customer's property, if for example you were incorporating it into your finished works (as a contractor I remember we had to include a customer's artwork in a reception installation). If you don't do this then you clearly don't need to say anything about it. Another example is "Design". Many, many construction specialists don't actually "Design" in terms of creating something brand new under the sun. When I worked for a specialist partitions and ceilings subcontractor for example we regularly "completed

Not Just a Tick in a Box 39

Chapter 5 — Quality Management

design" or offered "design detailing" but the crucial point was that we used our knowledge and skills to add "buildability" considerations to a design concept or a general specification. Moreover, the detailing that we would bring to the project would be proven manufacturer's solutions for the issue in hand, be it a junction or abutment detail or a performance solution. The "Design" of this input had obviously been created, tested and proven by the manufacturer not ourselves. This allowed us to legitimately exclude "Design" from our Scope of Registration. If and when you do exclude items you must state what you are excluding and why you are doing so. In my example our explanation for excluding "Design" was along the lines that we responded to architectural designs and specifications and brought proven manufacturer's solutions to the project where required.

So that was a quick look at the requirements of an effective Quality Management System as required by the International Standard ISO 9001. Is there anything in there that you would question as to its relevance for your business?

Summary

The Elements of a Quality Management System:

- Management Commitment
- Policy
- Quality Management Manual
- Roles and Responsibilities
- Competence
- Customer-Focused Processes
- Monitoring
- Review
- Continual Improvement

Environmental Management

The ISO 14000 family addresses various aspects of Environmental Management. It provides practical tools for companies and organisations looking to identify and control their environmental impact and constantly improve their environmental performance. ISO 14001:2004 and ISO 14004:2004 focus on Environmental Management Systems. The other Standards in the family focus on specific environmental aspects such as life cycle analysis, communication and auditing.

Again for our purposes as specialist construction contractors, we are looking for guidance on the criteria for an Environmental Management System and a Standard that our businesses can be certified to. ISO 14001:2004 is that document; the internationally recognised Standard for the Environmental Management of businesses. It prescribes controls for those activities that have an effect on the environment. These include the use of natural resources, handling and treatment of waste and energy consumption. It does not state requirements for environmental performance, but maps out a framework that a company or organisation can follow to set up an effective Environmental Management

Chapter 6 — Environmental Management

System. It can be used by any organisation regardless of its activity or sector. Using ISO 14001:2004 can provide assurance to company management and employees as well as external stakeholders (back to our PQQ's) that environmental impact is understood, is being measured and is being improved.

Some of the "green" benefits of using ISO 14001:2004 that are often cited include:

- reduced cost of waste management
- savings in consumption of energy and materials
- improved corporate image among regulators, customers and the public.

In the modern construction industry, contractors are charged with achieving and demonstrating sound environmental performance by controlling the impacts of their activities, products and services on the environment. The background context is one of increasingly stringent legislation, societal measures that foster environmental protection, and increased concern expressed by interested parties (main contractors, Local Authorities and end users) about environmental matters and sustainable development. Your business's capability to effectively manage its impact on the environment is rapidly becoming a non-negotiable requirement and can sometimes, on its own, be the differentiating factor between your bid and your competitors!

ISO 14001 specifies Requirements for an Environmental Management System to enable an organisation to develop and implement an Environmental Policy and Environmental Objectives which take into account legal requirements and information about an organisation's significant environmental aspects. It is intended to apply to all types and sizes of organisation and to accommodate diverse geographical, cultural and social conditions. "The overall aim of this

International Standard is to support environmental protection and prevention of pollution in balance with socio-economic needs". Demonstration of successful implementation of ISO 14001 provides that all important capability to assure interested parties that an appropriate environmental management system is in place (as advised above, ISO 14001 contains only those requirements that can be objectively audited, not specific environmental performance criteria).

Just as we did with ISO 9001, let's now look specifically at the Requirements of ISO 14001 in relation to a company's Environmental Management System.

General requirement of environmental management

ISO 14001 expects organisations to establish, document, implement, maintain and continually improve an Environmental Management System in accordance with its requirements and determine how it will fulfil these requirements.

Specific requirements of environmental management

Environmental policy

An appropriate (there goes my favourite word again) Environmental Policy is required which is the driver for implementing and improving the Environmental Management System so that the organisation can maintain and potentially improve its environmental performance. As you would expect given the Quality Management Principle of Leadership, the involvement of Top Management is inescapable and we are looking for commitment to the following via the **publicly** declared Environmental Policy Statement:

- compliance (for all practical purposes) with applicable legal and other requirements

Chapter 6 — Environmental Management

- preventing pollution

- continual improvement (!)

- setting objectives and targets to improve environmental performance

- ensuring the Environmental Management System is communicated and understood by internal and external interested parties

- periodically reviewing and revising the Environmental Management System and Policy to reflect changing conditions and information.

For ISO 14001, the Plan of Plan-Do-Check & Act starts with gaining an understanding of your business's effect on the environment and the legal framework under which you operate.

Environmental aspects and impacts

The organisation must identify and understand the environmental aspects (an "aspect" is defined as element of an organisation's activities or products or services that can interact with the environment and can be anything from use of power and water to waste generated) arising from its existing and/or planned activities, products and services, in order to determine the environmental impacts of significance and take them into account and control them when establishing the Environmental Management System. An understanding of a business's environmental impact needs to be demonstrated.

Legal requirements

The organisation needs to understand the legal and regulatory framework within which it operates, by identifying applicable legal requirements; especially ones pertinent to its environmental aspects, and other requirements to which the organisation subscribes and taking them into account in establishing the environmental management system. More than understanding the legal requirements the organisation should also be able to demonstrate that it has evaluated **compliance** with the legal requirements identified, including applicable permits or licences.

Objectives and targets

The Standard also requires the identification of priorities and the setting of appropriate Environmental Objectives and Targets. These should be specific and measurable, cover short and long-term issues, address specific elements of the organisation's operations and have a programme for their achievement and also, ideally, with someone identified as taking responsibility for doing do. Clearly if you have identified any significant environmental impacts and/or are concerned about some of the legal obligations you have identified then your Objectives and Targets should start with these areas.

Structure for implementation, for the do(ing) in Plan-Do-Check & Act

The successful implementation of an Environmental Management System calls for a commitment from all persons working for the organisation or on its behalf (including subcontractors) beginning, as we have seen, with the highest levels of management. A specific management representative(s) with defined responsibility **and authority** for implementing the Environmental Management System should be designated. Appropriate resources, such as organisational infrastructure, should be provided to ensure that the Environmental Management System is established, implemented and maintained. It is also important that the key environmental management system roles and responsibilities are well defined and communicated to all persons working for or on behalf of the organisation.

Competence, training and awareness

The organisation should identify the awareness, knowledge, understanding and skills needed by any person with the responsibility and authority to perform tasks relating to the Environmental Management System on its behalf. People, including subcontractors, need to be competent to perform the tasks, to which they are assigned, and training needs should be identified and actions taken to ensure the provision of training. All persons need to be aware of the organisation's Environmental Policy and Environmental Management System and the environmental aspects of the organisation's activities, products and services that could be affected by their work.

Communication

Communication is important to ensure awareness of and the effective implementation of the Environmental Management System and internal and external methods will be required. This can start with something as simple as posters in your office asking for lights and machines to be turned off at the end of the day, explanation of waste and recycling arrangements, to tool box talks on environmental issues on site.

Documentation control

The level of detail of the documentation should be sufficient to describe the Environmental Management System and how its parts work together, and to provide direction on where to obtain more detailed information on the operation of specific parts of it. The intent is to ensure that organisations create and maintain documents in a manner sufficient to implement the Environmental Management System. However, as always the primary focus of organisations should be on effective implementation of the system and on environmental performance, not on a complex document control system. Ask what your business needs and don't do anymore; remember, fit ISO to your business, don't expect your business to fit to ISO.

Operational control

An organisation should evaluate those of its operations that are associated

Chapter 6 — Environmental Management

with its identified significant environmental aspects and ensure that they are conducted in a way that will control or reduce the adverse impacts associated with them, in order to fulfil the requirements of its environmental policy and meet its Objectives and Targets. This should include all parts of its operations, including maintenance activities. This is where you implement controls that you have decided are necessary in relation to controlling and minimising the environmental impact of your activities that you have already recognised. These "controls" could well be very simple indeed and should be integrated with what you would normally do to deliver your product or service.

Emergency preparedness

It is the responsibility of each organisation to develop emergency preparedness and response procedures that suits its own particular needs. This is a feature common to the ISO family of Standards. In this instance we are looking for arrangements that will swing into action should an environmental emergency occur such as polluting a watercourse or inappropriate waste disposal.

To add to our obligation under ISO 14001 to ensure planning (Plan) and control (Do) of our Environmental Management we must add monitoring, preventive and corrective actions, auditing and review (Check and Act), to ensure that our policy is complied with and that the Environmental Management System remains appropriate.

Monitoring & measurement

The organisation should monitor and measure, on a regular basis, the key characteristics of its operations that can have a significant environmental impact, how it is achieving its Objectives and Targets, and improving its environmental performance.

What happens when things go wrong?

Depending on the nature of the issue or problem, the organisation needs to have measures in place for when something goes wrong. This can often be accomplished with a minimum of formal planning, or it may be a more complex and long-term activity. As always, any documentation should be appropriate (are you counting?) to the matter in hand, and would for example including a mechanism for investigating any environmental 'incidents'.

Internal audits

Internal audits are required and these can be performed by the organisation's own staff or by external personnel. As with all aspects of monitoring, the intent is ensure that the policy is complied with and that the Environmental Management System remains appropriate to the organisation's activities. Internal auditing is not a policing activity it is an opportunity to gauge effectiveness and seek recommendations for improvement.

Management review

Management Review is, as we have seen, another common feature of the ISO auditable Standards. This is led by Top Management and assesses whether the Environmental Management System continues to be suitable and effective for the Organisation. All areas of the System need to be reviewed periodically. The review will include the results of internal audits, assessment of the operation for the Environmental Management System and environmental performance, feedback from customers and interested parties, and also consider any changes to the organisation's operations that have impacted on the System. The System needs to be capable of adapting to changing circumstances.

Getting started

When considering developing an Environmental Management System the best starting point is a review to consider all current environmental aspects of the organisation. The review should cover four key areas:

1. Identification of environmental aspects and impacts

2. Identification of applicable legal requirements and other requirements

3. Examination of existing environmental management practices and procedures, including those associated with procurement and contracting activities

4. Evaluation of previous emergency situations and accidents.

Once a review is complete, comparison of the organisation's current position with the requirements of ISO 14001 can allow the formation of an action plan to close any gaps.

Why seek ISO 14001 Certification?

Once you have an Environmental Management System in place, you may choose to have it externally audited. This is your choice but I highly recommend it and following a successful audit by an accredited Certification Body, you will be issued with a Certificate of Registration to ISO 14001. This demonstrates that your organisation is committed to environmental issues and is prepared to work towards improving the environment. It also gives a competitive edge to the company's marketing and enhances its image in the eyes of customers, employees and shareholders.

Chapter 6 — Summary

Summary

Fundamentals of an Environmental Management System:

- Management Commitment
- Environmental Policy
- Environmental Management Manual
- Roles and Responsibilities
- Competence
- Awareness of and Control of Environmental Impact
- Awareness of Legal Framework
- Environmentally-Focused Processes
- Monitoring
- Review
- Continual Improvement

Occupational Health & Safety Management

Organisations of all kinds are increasingly concerned with achieving and demonstrating sound Occupational Health & Safety performance. Furthermore, this is against a background of increasingly stringent legislation and increased concern expressed by interested parties about Occupational Health & Safety issues. OHSAS (Occupational Health & Safety Assessment Series) 18001 has been developed in response to the demand for a recognisable Occupational Health & Safety Management System Standard against which management systems can be assessed and certified. Safety "reviews" or "audits" on their own may not be sufficient to provide an organisation with the assurance that its performance not only meets, but will continue to meet, its legal and policy requirements. To be effective, they need to be conducted within a structured management system that is integrated within the organisation.

OHSAS 18001 specifies requirements for such an Occupational Health & Safety (OH&S) Management System. These Requirements will enable an organisation to develop an Occupational Health & Safety Policy, control its risks, establish objectives and processes to achieve the policy commitments and take action as needed to improve its performance.

Chapter 7 — Occupational Health & Safety Management

Demonstration of successful implementation of this OHSAS Standard, via Certification by a UKAS Accredited Body, can be used by businesses to assure (we are seeing again and again that such assurance is a benefit of the Standards and recognising one of the main reasons for PQQ's) their customers that an appropriate OH&S Management System is in place. 18001 does not state specific Occupational Health & Safety performance criteria, nor does it give detailed specifications for the design of a management system. In structure, OHSAS 18001 is similar to ISO 14001 as I am sure you will recognise. You will also by now recognise the Plan-Do-Check & Act process methodology and also the presence of the Eight Quality Management Principles. Like 9001 and 14001, 18001 uses the word "shall" to be specific about what is required, as you will see below. While 18001 goes beyond the requirements of schemes such as CHAS and is recognised as the gold standard in relation to Health & Safety management, any controls that you have developed for the likes of CHAS will put you well on the way to tacking the requirements of OHSAS 18001.

General requirement

The organisation shall establish, document, implement, maintain and continually improve an OH&S Management System in accordance with the requirements of 18001 and determine how it will fulfil these requirements.

Specific requirements

Occupational health & safety policy

Top Management (**Leadership**), as always, shall define and authorise an appropriate (!) Occupational Health & Safety Policy that commits the organisation to:

- the prevention of injury and ill health

- continual improvement in OH&S management and OH&S performance

- to at least complying with applicable legal requirements

- setting and reviewing OH&S objectives.

The Policy needs to be:

- communicated to all persons working under the control of the organisation with the intent that they are made aware of their individual Occupational Health & Safety obligations (so this will obviously include any subcontractors working for you)

- available to interested parties, your customers for example who will ask for your Occupational Health & Safety Policy from time to time

- reviewed periodically to ensure that it remains relevant and appropriate to the organisation.

Planning

The organisation shall establish, implement and maintain a procedure for the ongoing hazard identification, risk assessment, and determination of necessary controls and OHSAS 18001 further instructs and advises how this should be done.

Legal and other requirements

The organisation shall establish, implement and maintain a procedure for identifying, accessing and applying the legal and other Occupational Health & Safety requirements that are applicable to it. Just as with ISO 14001, what we are looking for here is a demonstration of both the understanding and applicability of the legal framework.

Evaluation of compliance

Consistent with its commitment to compliance, the organisation shall establish, implement and maintain a procedure for periodically evaluating compliance with applicable legal requirements. This is easily done and a variety of help is available.

Objectives and targets

The organisation shall establish, implement and maintain documented Occupational Health & Safety Objectives and targets, at relevant functions and levels within the organisation with an accompanying programme and designated responsibility. This should prove to be a powerful improvement exercise.

Implementation and operation, responsibility, accountability and authority

Top Management shall take ultimate responsibility for Occupational Health & Safety and the OH&S Management System and demonstrate its commitment by resource provision, allocating responsibilities and accountabilities, and appointing a member of Top Management with specific responsibility for Occupational Health & Safety and the OH&S Management System.

Competence, training and awareness

The organisation shall ensure that any person under its control performing tasks that can impact on Occupational Health & Safety is competent on the basis of appropriate education, training or experience, and shall retain associated records. The organisation shall further identify, provide and evaluate training to raise people to the relevant and appropriate levels of competence. As we have seen with our overviews of Quality and Environmental Management, demonstrable competence of your people to perform the roles that are allocated is a fundamental ISO Principle.

Communication, participation and consultation

The organisation shall establish, implement and maintain a procedure for internal and external communication with, participation of, and consultation with all staff in relation to Occupational Health & Safety matters. It is important that your staff are given the opportunity to be consulted and to participate in your Health & Safety arrangements.

Documentation

Documents are of course required but It is important that documentation is proportional to the level of complexity, hazards and risks concerned and is kept to the minimum required for effectiveness and efficiency. This will at least include OH&S Policy and Objectives; description of the main elements of the OH&S Management System and their interaction, and reference to related documents and records necessary to ensure the effective planning, operation and control of processes that relate to the management of its Occupational Health & Safety risks.

Control of documents and records

To maintain the integrity of the OH&S Management System documents need to be "controlled" in the sense that the right documents are available and used at the right time, and records need to be readily identifiable and retrievable.

Operational control

The organisation shall determine those operations and activities that are associated with the identified hazards where the implementation of controls is necessary to manage the Occupational Health & Safety risk, for example controls related to purchased goods, equipment and services and controls related to contractors and other visitors to the workplace.

Emergency preparedness and response

The organisation shall establish, implement and maintain emergency procedures both for office premises and site activities.

Performance measurement and monitoring

The organisation shall establish, implement and maintain a procedure to monitor and measure Occupational Health & Safety performance on a regular basis including qualitative and quantitative measures, monitoring objectives and monitoring the effectiveness of controls.

Incident investigation

Should Health & Safety accidents and incidents occur the organisation shall fully investigate and analyse them in order to determine causes and take whatever action is necessary to prevent recurrence and identify opportunities for preventive action and continual improvement.

Nonconformity, corrective action and preventive action

As always with ISO there is a need for the organisation to establish, implement and maintain a procedure for dealing with actual and potential nonconformity (i.e. something going wrong) and for taking corrective action and preventive action. The organisation shall ensure that any necessary changes arising from corrective action and preventive action are made to the OH&S Management System documentation.

Internal audit

The organisation shall ensure that internal audits of the OH&S Management System are conducted at planned intervals. The purpose of internal audits is to assess conformity to your planned arrangements for Occupational Health & Safety management, and proper implementation and effectiveness in meeting the organisation's Policy and Objectives. In other words, do you do what you say you do and is it effective? 18001 provides guidance on how this should be done.

Management review

Top Management shall review the organisation's OH&S Management System, at planned intervals, to ensure its continuing suitability, adequacy and effectiveness. This is an important exercise and represents another major improvement opportunity. Reviews shall include assessing opportunities for improvement and the need for changes to the OH&S Management System, including the OH&S Policy and OH&S Objectives.

The Review will include the following:

- results of internal audits and evaluations of compliance

- results of participation and consultation

- relevant communication from external interested parties, including complaints

- the OH&S performance of the organisation

- the extent to which objectives have been met

- the status of incident investigations, corrective actions and preventive actions

- follow-up actions from previous Management Reviews

- changing circumstances, including developments in legal and other requirements related to Occupational Health & Safety

- recommendations for improvement.

Chapter 7 — Occupational Health & Safety Management

A powerful exercise I am sure you will agree to ensure that you are on top of your Health & Safety Management.

Hopefully you are noticing the recurrent themes of the Eight Quality Management Principles and the common way each Standard strives to include them.

Summary

Fundamentals of a Occupational Health & Safety Management System:

- Management Commitment
- OH&S Policy
- OH&S Manual
- Roles and Responsibilities
- Competence
- Awareness of and Control of Health & Safety Risks
- Awareness of Legal Framework
- OH&S-Focused Processes
- Monitoring
- Review
- Continual Improvement

8

PAS2030

As mentioned in the introduction to this book I have decided to include a section on PAS2030, the required Certification for installers under the Green Deal, for a variety of reasons:

- The Green Deal will go from strength to strength in spite of its spluttering start in some regions and work will therefore become available to a variety of construction specialists; but only if they are certified to PAS2030

- PAS2030 embodies a variety of ISO Principles and Requirements and I wanted to show the similarity to reinforce the relevance of ISO to construction specialists

- Contractors will need to become certified to PAS2030 whether or not they are ISO certified

- Fortunately for those who **are** ISO certified, the Requirements of PAS2030 sit nicely within an ISO-compliant Integrated Management System

- I am currently assisting some contractors to secure PAS2030 Certification and seeing at first-hand how it is opening up new customers and markets for them (one of the most common reasons cited by my ISO customers is "to open up new markets and customers"!)

- PAS2030 demands the development of a highly specific Quality Management System in order to effectively execute and control its requirements.

Some introductory remarks first

The Green Deal is a market framework based on a key principle that some energy efficiency related changes to properties pay for themselves, in effect, through the resulting savings on fuel bills. It creates a financing mechanism that will allow a range of energy efficiency measures to be installed in both dwellings and non-dwellings at no upfront cost.

The primary objective for the PAS 2030 is the provision of a robust, uniformly applicable framework (Quality Management System) that will assist installers that comply with its requirements in full to demonstrate that their installation processes are capable of providing installation of energy efficiency improvement measures to manufacturer's and best practice specification and in accordance with the customer's expectations. Unlike ISO, PAS2030 is very prescriptive i.e. there are practices you simply have to comply with in order to secure Certification. These are not difficult to do for the competent specialist, I just make the point that there is not so much discretion as there is with ISO. Conversely, some of PAS's prescriptions may be sufficiently attractive to you in order to control your projects that you may want to replicate them when performing non-Green Deal works.

The Department of Energy and Climate Change

The DECC uses PAS 2030:

- to set the requirements for the installation of the measure(s) under the Green Deal and in accordance with the requirements of the Green Deal Code of Practice

- as a good practice benchmark for installations carried out on their flagship policy.

PAS 2030 is structured with a common set of requirements which the installer has to meet and then these are supplemented by the specific demands of each Energy Efficiency Measure (EEM) to be installed which are set out in Annexes.

Therefore, the best way to satisfy the requirements of PAS 2030 is to develop a simple Quality Management System which embodies a process to follow (**A System Approach to Management!**).

Specific requirements

The Requirements can be reduced to the following sequential process:

- Decide whether or not to tender based on an assessment of your resources and capabilities — this is of course similar to ISO's demand that you fully understand your customer's requirements and ensure that at a high level somebody has objectively decided that you are capable of meeting those requirements

Chapter 8 — PAS2030

- If the decision is positive commence an Installation Process Control procedure to demonstrate your compliance to PAS2030 for start to finish, just as you might have a checklist for your own ISO control procedures

- Conduct a Pre-Installation Survey if applicable — a specific PAS requirement either by a main contractor or a specialist

- Develop a comprehensive Method Statement for the work — standard OHSAS 18001 fare but PAS is more prescriptive

- Ensure your operatives have the necessary competence to install the EEM in question — we have already discovered that Competence is a fundamental ISO Principle

- Ensure you have the necessary competence and resources at supervisory level — ditto, but again PAS is very prescriptive

- Execute your works with adequate quality assurance checks — need I add anything?

- Have a mechanism to confirm and record variations — as you would under any construction project

- Have a mechanism to record and learn from feedback from your operatives — while this is not a prescriptive item of ISO it is of course consistent with internal auditing and continual improvement

- Ensure an effective handover process, again more prescriptive under PAS but something you obviously want in an Integrated Management System

Chapter 8 — PAS2030

- Conduct internal audits of your PAS2030 operations, one of ISO's major compliance and improvement processes

- Retain adequate records of your PAS2030 operations, a Mandatory Procedure under ISO 9001 but again very prescriptive here

- Ensure customer service requirements are adhered to, this incudes complaints handling and interaction with customers just as it would under ISO

- Make a declaration of PAS2030 Conformity, which is unique to PAS and has to be made for every installation.

Quite clearly therefore a Quality Management System to ensure PAS conformance adds to and is supported by an ISO compliant Quality Management System. Might as well integrate them, don't you think?

Chapter 8 — Summary

Summary

Fundamentals of a PAS2030 Quality Management System:

- Management Commitment

- PAS Policy

- PAS Quality Management Manual

- Competence

- Process Control

- Declaration of Conformity

- Monitoring

- Review

- Continual Improvement

Get Integrated

We have looked at the requirements of ISO 9001, ISO 14001 and OHSAS 18001, and indeed PAS2030, and we will go on to look at how to build a compliant management system. I am sure you have noticed that there are obvious similarities in some of the requirements of the Standards. In fact, for 9001, 14001 and 18001 about a third of the Standards are almost word-for-word the same. Furthermore, 14001 and 18001 follow the same structure. PAS is a little different in that, albeit based on ISO Principles, it is far more prescriptive because as we have seen it has been designed for a particular situation.

All the Standards that concern us as construction specialists can be successfully combined to form an Integrated Management System (IMS). ISO 9001 is undoubtedly the bedrock; while 14001 and 18001 have been designed to both standalone and to combine with or bolt on to ISO 9001. PAS sits nicely within an Integrated Management System especially as it has elements in common with 9001 and its unique prescriptive elements can easily sit in the "Doing" section as operational procedures. In fact, ISO wraps nicely around PAS2030 and the prescriptive elements of PAS2030 can be used to inform elements of ISO.

Chapter 9 — Get Integrated

The most successful Integrated Management System framework takes ISO 9001 as the basis. The common elements of ISO 9001, ISO 14001 and OHSAS 18001 are dealt with simultaneously. The unique elements of 14001 and 18001 are added in according to where they arise within the Plan-Do-Check & Act sequence.

The elements of PAS that are quintessentially ISO 9001, will have already been dealt with; its unique operational elements can be satisfied within the Integrated Management System's implementation and operation section. This is exactly what we did with Coen Ltd. Coen were certified to PAS2030 in October 2012 and to 9001/14001/18001 in January 2013 but from the outset the intention was to develop an Integrated Management System for all the business's operations. The chronology of the Certification was purely down to the customer's and operational requirements. Doing an enormous amount of External Wall Insulation over the summer and autumn of 2012 Coen were abruptly asked to secure PAS Certification to satisfy their customer's own obligations. At the PAS assessment, the assessors were presented with an IMS that had addressed all the requirements of PAS with some standalone items and other items such as PAS internal audits, and PAS complaints procedures included in the overall IMS section of internal auditing and customer feedback/complaints handling. Some of the ISO Requirements beyond PAS had not been fully developed at that time of the PAS assessment but the developing IMS was still the vehicle chosen to demonstrate readiness for PAS Certification. Coen passed PAS first time.

You will know right from the start of this book that I always encourage my customers to choose to develop an Integrated Management System from the outset; even if they have no experience of developing management systems and are starting from scratch. If you have the mind-set to achieve ISO 9001, you can add the others with not much more of a stretch. Far from being more complex, it can actually prove easier to begin with the end of an integrated system in mind rather than developing three systems with the intention of integrating them at a later date. There are obvious immediate benefits to going for an IMS, not least the elimination of duplication among the Standards.

The time and cost saving can be substantial in the preparation phase, whether you engage a consultant or not. Requirements of all three Standards can be satisfied by one procedure within your manual. Specific operational activities, such as risk assessments for example, can tackle Health & Safety and Environmental risks within the one assessment. You can also for example document your site manager's Health & Safety and Environmental responsibilities at the same time.

The time and cost saving when it comes to auditing can be even more favourable. Certification bodies will happily visit you on three separate occasions to audit your Quality Management System, then your Environmental Management System and then your Occupational Health & Safety Management System, and happily charge you for the privilege on each occasion. The time taken to audit can legitimately be reduced substantially under UKAS rules when there is a properly Integrated Management System.

Tackling an IMS from the outset compels you to think holistically about your business. We said earlier that no modern construction projects are divorced from Quality, Health & Safety and Environmental issues. Your customers demand that you address all three areas from the tender onwards. In fact, even before that. Have you ever seen a PQQ that did not enquire about your Environmental competence? Or omitted questions about your Health & Safety capabilities? Your site team cannot avoid your customer's high expectations of a Quality installation with Health & Safety and Environmental management taken for granted.

When that is the case why not develop an IMS that aims high from the start gun and uses the Requirements of the Standards to drive best practice in all three areas of Quality Management, Environmental Management and Occupational Health & Safety Management?

Chapter 9 — Get Integrated

The operational benefits of doing so will be even greater. For your site teams the need to deliver quality is so essential as to be beyond discussion. Only excellence in final installation satisfies these days. Similarly, over the last twenty years the industry has made enormous strides in improving Health & Safety performance. RAMS, near-miss reporting, appropriate PPE, plant control and inspections, and Health & Safely proactivity are no-brainers also. Environmental Management has a little way to go but is so high profile that it is only a matter of, a probably very short, time. The sooner your whole team thinks Quality/Environmental/Safety instinctively the better for your business. Engaging your team to develop an Integrated Management System will be a massive impetus to that very necessary process.

Summary

Fundamentals of an Integrated Management System:

- Manage all your business operations in one Management System
- Satisfy the common elements of 9001/14001/18001 at the same time, eliminating duplication
- Think Quality/Environment/Health & Safety in everything you do
- Add unique 14001 and 18001 elements appropriately to the Plan-Do-Check & Act sequence
- Monitoring
- Review
- Continual Improvement

10

Show Me The Benefits

Chapter 10 — Show Me The Benefits

I talk about the benefits of ISO Certification throughout this book and this chapter additionally serves to pull together some of the benefits most often cited by certified organisations and also offer my own views which include some benefits not often mentioned by others.

A focus on quality is clearly vital for sustaining your business and also for providing new opportunities from quality installations. Certification to ISO 9001 makes a powerful statement to your customers, and your wider community, that you are serious about quality delivery. There are many business benefits cited by those who have secured Certification, by their customers and of course by the ISO organisation itself which has conducted many in-depth studies.

So let's look at what others say about the benefits, as securing Certification will demand some time, effort and money. In fact it can take lots of all three if done improperly and we will look at that later.

We will look at the best way to implement the Standards in order to gain and maximise these benefits in chapter 14 so here we will just look at the benefits that organisations cite.

Hopefully, when reading through the Requirements of the Standards in previous chapters, you will have appreciated that some of the benefits are already obvious.

Improved product and service quality and consistency from 9001's compulsion to determine and, in some form, document what you consider to be your Best Practice; **Increased customer satisfaction levels** — from the Customer Focus demanded by 9001. Which of course leads to **higher retention rate of existing customers** and the holy of grail of customer satisfaction: repeat business from customers who are confident of your ability to deliver! **Improved productivity, less waste, fewer mistakes** and costs of abortive and corrective work — from doing things right first time, from clarity of purpose, from following your best practice.

Chapter 10 — Show Me The Benefits

We have mentioned the joys of PPQ's a few times already but it is unavoidable these days that many main contractors and other major organisations such as Local Authorities insist on a company having ISO 9001 Certification (and other Standards) in order to achieve "preferred supplier" status, or simply to be allowed to tender for their business in the first place. In some sectors, ISO Certification is a contractual obligation. A major UK contractor currently also insists on ISO 14001 Certification. I have spoken to a few main contractors about their use of PPQ's and their supply chain selection criteria in general and they tell me that the questions they ask of us subcontractors are the same questions that their customers are asking of them! So we can add to our list of obvious benefits of Certification:

The opportunity to tender for new contracts — by satisfying pre-qualification criteria

Enhanced chances of preferred supplier status — when Certification is a prerequisite of moving up the supply chain; these first two reasons thereby offering competitive advantage over those without ISO Certification

For lots of my customers the initial motivation to secure Certification is indeed to gain access to a new customer or new market by satisfying pre-qualification criteria. This is perfectly legitimate and is such an obvious benefit that for some businesses this is enough — to get on more tender lists and win more business.

New customers cannot know everything about you but Quality Management Standards like ISO 9001 can "signal" the quality of your business — the whole point of PPQ's is for your customer to be assured that you are a safe pair of hands. So it is believed that your ISO 9001 certificate itself will provide benefits by **"signalling" quality** and some of my customers will testify to this.

Chapter 10 — Show Me The Benefits

Getting on tender lists and winning more tenders is one thing; executing your projects at a profit is another. Comfortingly, another benefit cited, by many organisations, from ISO Certification is:

Increased profitability (both increased revenue and reduced costs)

Studies and analysis by the ISO do in fact show that 9001 Certification enhances financial performance and that increased sales is the initial reason bolstered by external benefits such as customer satisfaction and "signalling" benefits just mentioned.

I of course urge you to accept that, beyond getting onto tender lists, the real value of Certification is the **business improvement** that it will bring year on year if the Standards are embraced and used properly and effectively. Interestingly, the initial motivation for seeking Certification has been found to effect financial performance. External pressure from customers and markets is, as I have previously agreed, a sound reason but those who are serious about real quality improvement in all business operations will enjoy greater overall benefits.

Successfully getting onto tender lists is a quick fix and it would be a shame to leave it at that. Embracing the Standards, and applying the Quality Management Principles to all areas of your day-to-day operations will drive quality and ensure effective implementation and significant performance, including financial performance, benefits. (The ISO's studies looked at certified organisations against similar but non-certified, and looked at return on assets, sales, investment and equity, and profit margin, profitability, increased sales and market share).

As well as improvements to management and business performance my customers also cite:

Chapter 10 — Show Me The Benefits

Enhanced professional status as an enjoyable benefit of Certification; **Pride in their businesses** is a very common characteristic of those who seek Certification and it is immensely rewarding for me to see individuals and business elevated by securing Certification and the massive statement of intent that provides. Why not? Certification means differentiation and proven business credentials.

Increased motivation and morale of your staff is yet another often cited benefit. This is not hard to understand given the Standards' compulsion to ensure your people are not only demonstrably competent to perform their roles but are also clear of where they fit into and contribute to your business.

All the above benefits discussed so far have a Quality Management dimension but can equally be applied as benefits of ISO 14001 and OHSAS 18001 also. What's more, these Standards have unique benefits of their own.

Having an ISO 14001 Environmental Management System, whether standalone or part of an Integrated Management System, will make a powerful statement to all your stakeholders about your organisation's **commitment to the environment** and give you internationally recognised **"Green Credentials"**. Green contracting is one of the highest profile current initiatives in construction and pressure, quite rightly, emanates from the top, from building owners and users. Don't you think the "Environmental" section of the dreaded PPQ's is getting bigger and more demanding? The CITB states the most comprehensive way to manage your environmental impact and performance is to develop an Environmental Management System certified to ISO 14001.

The increasingly stringent background of environmental legislation is not to be under-estimated. There are already construction-related convictions in place. While it is not the job of a 14001 Auditor to tell you whether or not you comply with the law, the ISO 14001 Standard does compel you, as we have seen, to **understand the regulatory framework** within which you operate and

Chapter 10 — Show Me The Benefits

have plans in place to make sure that you do not transgress. When combined with the equal need to understand how your operations impact upon the environment then you certainly have a powerful mechanism to **manage your environmental risks**.

ISO 14001 and OHSAS 18001 have risk management at their heart and the immediate benefit you should see is a **reduction in insurance premiums**! By securing Certification you have just instilled Environmental and Health & Safety risk management into your business so if you do not get a reduction in your insurance premiums then change your insurance company. Other cost savings will result as continual improvement drives efficiency and improved Environmental Management.

Obviously the same holds true for your OHSAS 18001 Occupational Health & Safety Management System. Through 18001 Certification you will have demonstrated that you have a **structured approach to hazard identification**

Chapter 10 — Show Me The Benefits

and understand your Health & Safety risks, have adequate and effective measures in place to control them, and also **understand the Health & Safety laws under which you operate** and have arrangements to comply with them. All with a view to risk mitigation. And mitigating **your** risks also goes a long way to mitigating your Customer's risks and increases your chances of selection.

Just as 14001 Certification displays your "Green Credentials" then Certification to 18001 is a clear and bold statement to your staff and to your customers about not only your **commitment to Health & Safety** but also your commitment to improving health and safety performance through **objectives and targets.**

18001 Certification will mean that you have **clearly defined Health & Safely responsibilities** in your organisation and are better placed to **safeguard the wellbeing of your staff and your business** and **prevent ill health, injury and accidents with resulting reduction in downtime.**

So that's what successfully certified businesses are saying.

For me the fundamental benefit of ISO Certification is to have a set of Requirements to fulfil that will **guarantee a quality product** or service if implemented correctly. To have activities to execute that focuses your mind on proven routes to customer satisfaction. To have a System written by excellent business brains to guide you. This is not of course to say that we can't run our businesses without such guidance but that smart money has written these Standards and equally smart money has implemented them successfully to the enormous benefits of their businesses.

These are International Standards that represent the ultimate in Quality Management, Environmental Management and Occupational Health & Safety Management. Other people have worked all that out, leaving you to concentrate on the unique features of your service.

Chapter 10 — Show Me The Benefits

When you secure Certification to the Standards, you have completed a process that focuses your mind on customer satisfaction. It compels you to determine what best practice means to you, and encourages you to put processes in place to give you every chance of delivering best practice consistently. You have been guided on managing your risks. You have been made to think about the competence, training and morale of your staff. You have had to think about your key performance indicators, about what you need to measure to make sure that the business is functioning as you wish. And you will have built in to your operations monitoring and review processes to ensure that you continually improve. What do you measure and monitor at the moment? What improvement activities do you currently undertake?

So in my view, one of the greatest benefits of seeking ISO Certification is **the act of developing your quality or integrated management system itself and how it makes you really think about how you do things.** Even greater benefits are to be had from then embracing the Standards and their activities in order to steadily build long-term value into your business.

So ideally, and critically for success, the decision to develop a Quality Management System and seek independent Certification should be a strategic one. ISO 9001 itself says so from the outset. The effort and commitment involved to strive for real quality improvements from superior customer-focused service are not to be taken lightly but are of course perfectly achievable if you are serious. We'll look at how to do it in chapter 14 but before we do we really need to look at the **myths** surrounding ISO and its implementation. There have been plenty of horror stories surrounding implementation which have contributed to some "bad press". I think it is important that we debunk these myths before we look at how to, and how not to do it.

Summary

Benefits:

- Statement of intent to your customers
- Improved product or service quality
- Increased customer satisfaction
- Higher customer retention rates
- Improved productivity
- Less waste, fewer mistakes
- Opportunity to tender new contracts
- Enhanced chances of preferred supplier status
- Assured safe pair of hands
- Increased profitability
- Business improvement and growth
- Enhanced professional status
- Pride in the business

Chapter 10 — Summary

- Increased staff motivation and morale
- Ideal cost-effective new-staff induction and training document
- Commitment to the Environment and Health & Safety
- Structured approach to understanding and managing your Environment and Health & Safety Risks
- Reduction in insurance premiums
- Safe guarding the wellbeing of your staff and business
- Guaranteed quality products or services
- How the act of developing a Quality Management System or IMS makes you really think about how you do things

11

Geek Mythology

ISO is shrouded in myths and misconceptions. A common theme is that "quality management" or developing a "quality management system" will be bureaucratic, involve lots of paperwork and is best suited to some geeky or nerdy person who loves admin.

Here are just some of the things that have been said to me on initial visits with customers:

"It will cost a fortune"

"It will tie us up in a straightjacket"

"It's too bureaucratic"

"Paperwork won't get the job built Andrew"

"We're too small to have a Quality Manager, that's for the big boys"

Chapter 11 — Geek Mythology

"We'll need loads of training to run it properly, I spend enough on training"

"There's only a few of us in the business"

"We'll need loads more people to run something like that"

"I don't want to have to write down everything that we do, that will take for ever"

"You need someone who loves paperwork; I'd never get my lot to do it"

"None of us can write -articulate — a QM"

"We're too busy; I can't spare anyone for that"

"The job is stressful enough without having to operate a quality management system"

"It will take too long"

"All the clause references confuse me"

"Can't stand all the jargon"

"Our customers are not asking for it"

"It will cost a fortune"

Well sometimes it does but it certainly should not! I do hear horror stories about high priced consultants charging some extortionate day rate and being there for ever. When I set up Foy Certification I intended to pitch against the market and as an ex-contractor who abhorred fixers working on "Daywork" I offered a fixed price to guide contractors to ISO Certification and I also guaranteed success. That has sometimes backfired for me when some customers have taken much

Chapter 11 — Geek Mythology

longer — for myriad reasons — than I anticipated but I still think it is the right thing to do. My customers have cost-certainty and that is important. When some people say "It is expensive" then of course the question is "Expensive when compared to what?" I help my customers to get there — with a guarantee remember — for the cost of a couple of fancy laptops. Now I would say this wouldn't I but I think that represents tremendous value when you consider the potential benefits — including return to the bottom line. Nobody can ever put a financial figure on the benefits of ISO but I think you would agree that enshrining practices that assure your customers, improve your business and manage your risks is potentially massive. And is that not worth a modest investment in a good consultant? Of course you can do it yourself, without my or anybody else's help, but then the question becomes the cost of your time against the cost of using a consultant to help you. If you are starting from scratch then you will inevitably need time to not only read the Standards but assimilate them in order to effectively apply them to your business. All that needs to be weighed up against the certain cost of using a consultant, if of course they offer a fixed price with a guarantee. And remember, the sooner you set up your management system and use it, the more cost savings you will enjoy. The ROI will be very quick. The value to the business of continual improvement is potentially enormous so does that sound expensive now?

"It will tie us up in a straightjacket"

I can only assume that this misconception comes from a belief that once you have a documented quality management system you have to follow it slavishly. Well assuming you have done the job properly wouldn't you want to follow it because it represents what best practice means to you? Of course you would but nothing is ever cast in stone. You have to be watchful for the integrity of your system in the sense that any changes must be controlled and effected properly - you cannot have a free-for-all with staff changing documents and procedures willy-nilly — but you want all your users challenging the system for effectiveness and suitability all the time. I used to encourage everyone to constantly challenge the manual we had created in terms of constantly asking can we do this better. Are these the most effective methods that we can come up with? Your quality management system is not a straightjacket; it is your agreed way of doing things at this moment in time, i.e. at this stage in your business's development given your current range of products and services, your current customer base and the client and market environments you operate in. There are lots of internal and external influences that may demand changes to your quality management system. ISO regularly compels you to ask if your quality management system is suitable and effective. If it is not you change it accordingly and make sure it is serving your business. There is always value in reviewing and assessing your quality management system's relevance! It is not a straightjacket; it is loose clothing to be adapted, amended or cast aside and start again in dramatic circumstances. Moreover, should crises occur or more changes occur in your business's scenario then ISO expects you to keep your system up to date.

Chapter 11 — Geek Mythology

"It's too bureaucratic"

This is another comment from the "paperwork" School of Objections. Nobody wants to build bureaucracy into their quality management system and you do have to be on guard to prevent it creeping in. It again comes down to the nature and level of control you need to deliver for your product or service. Some level of record keeping and sign-off is usually necessary and beneficial. By being vigilant as you develop your quality management system you can prevent bureaucratic creep. And as your system evolves, as it will, and often grows in size, as it will, the same vigilance will keep it in check. If procedures start to get complex and more paperwork looks like creeping in go back to the maxim that nothing gets into your quality management system unless it demonstrably adds to control of operations and consistency of quality delivery. Control forms can be multi-faceted if you wish, serving a number of activities simultaneously. As long as clarity is maintained always strive to kill two birds with one stone.

There are other reasons why an impression of bureaucracy emerges. Lots of people have heard horror stories about ISO 9001 implementation. This normally involves businesses who have files and files of procedures, work instructions, records and forms (generally sat on a shelf gathering dust) and have been trying to implement ISO 9001 for years unsuccessfully. To really ram the pain home they have spent a fortune doing so. Another common scenario is that of a quality manager who "wrote" a quality management system for them and then left. Because he had been operating in isolation, no other employee knew how to continue the process. Some businesses have gone through more than one quality manager each of them redefining, and adding to the last guy's efforts. Often this means changing a few things around as well which only adds to the fun. In spite of all this however, some businesses cling on to what has been produced, even in its muddled incoherent state and try to make it work, which just leads to more frustration and an ever worsening impression of 9001 and so-called "quality management" when it is all about poor, ill-led, confused implementation and nothing to do with the Standard itself. In these circumstances, starting again with a good consultant and/or a planned and systematic approach really is the most cost-effective way forward.

"Paperwork won't get the job built Andrew"

Initially, some of the sternest resistors to quality management systems and the inevitable, even if minimum, paperwork they necessitate are fixers and tradesmen. Guys of great practical skill are sometimes oblivious at first to anything that involves "pen pushing" and cannot see, or choose not to see,

Chapter 11 — Geek Mythology

the importance of for example demonstrable QA checks and Handovers to customers. I would have retired long ago had I a pound for every time someone told me, when explaining a modicum of necessary documentation, that "paperwork doesn't get the job built". I totally accept that and firmly believe that quality tradesmen are the be all and end all of quality installations. But in the modern construction industry and increasingly with private clients, verifiable quality assurance procedures are the norm. Is there anything more frustrating than doing a job twice because it never got handed over properly and got damaged before the customer "accepted" it? Verifiable QA procedures protect you and your work as well as giving assurance to the customers. They may not physically get the job built, of course not, but they are integral to completing the job, hopefully right first time. They are increasingly vital to getting paid as well. What's the point of being the best craftsmen in the world if your customer won't take responsibility for the work and pay your for it.

"We're too small to have a quality manager, that's for the big boys"

Who said you had to have a quality manager? Most of my customers do not. It is not a cliché to say that quality assurance is everyone's job. There is also the danger, and I have seen this happen, that having a "Quality Manager" results in everyone else relaxing and thinking that quality has nothing to do with them but is "his job". Your quality management system or integrated management system will cover your whole business from understanding what your customer needs, reviewing and defining those needs, delivering what is required, assessing your performance and ensuring customer satisfaction. There is clearly more to it than the activities of a quality manager. Also, when can any business be too small to want to instil assurance for their customers and business improvement procedures? I would argue that small businesses need a "system" which highlights the right things to do as it is very often the case that when people wear a number of "hats" they are pulled in a dozen different directions and find themselves often just reacting to events, the tyranny of the urgent, rather than concentrating on key activities. One of my customers is a two-man business (plus of course various subcontractors etc. and outsourced activities) who we managed to get successfully certified to ISO 9001, ISO 14001 and OHAS 18001 within an Integrated Management System. The trick, as always, was to develop a simple and effective system that served the business and did not need anything or anyone beyond the two guys to run it effectively. A small business needs a "small" management system, that is the point. You don't need to copy Virgin's operating procedures if you are a three man Drylining business, and ISO doesn't expect you to. Your system should be appropriate!

"We'll need loads of training to run it properly, I spend enough on training"

Why will you need loads of training? If your quality management system has been developed by fitting ISO to your business rather than fitting your business to ISO (see how I stuck that one in there) there will be little training to do. Furthermore,

Chapter 11 – Geek Mythology

if you have involved as many of your people as possible in developing your quality management system (something I urge you to do) then the need for training is reduced further. It's your system and you and your people have developed it so why do you need training in it? Yes, there will most probably be some ISO activities that are relatively new to you and will need to explained but if you accept that they will be concerned with either customer assurance, business improvement or risk management then, going back to an earlier theme of mine, you can't argue with that can you? Moreover, once you have your quality management system developed it becomes the ideal document to induct and train new staff. And I bet using your lean effective quality management system to induct and train staff will be very productive and cost-effective.

"There's only a few of us in the business"

We touched on this earlier with the myth that a business might be too small for ISO. Any business needs to manage its risks and consistently assure its customers. And we discussed earlier that unless you are improving you are deteriorating. Who is looking after these essential prerequisites for survival in a business with only a "few" people? It takes some discipline to ensure that they happen and arguably a quality management system with those disciplines enshrined is the easiest way to make sure they do.

"We'll need loads more people to run something like that"

This one always baffles me. Just as I said earlier that any Quality management system that adds stress to the job has completely missed the point, I would say the same about any quality management system that needs an army of people to administer it. Or even one more person. The aim right from the start is to enshrine good, preferably best practices that consistently deliver quality products and services.

Chapter 11 — Geek Mythology

That doesn't and shouldn't automatically lead to a layer of bureaucracy that needs more staff; in fact it absolutely should not do so. Everyone can play their part and it can be part of everyone's routine activities to ensure best practice. Of course there are some maintenance activities for any quality management system and these are vital but if, as you are developing your quality management system, they start to become demanding or unwieldy and cry out for additional staff then you have clearly gone down the wrong route. The art as always is to develop the leanest most practical and efficient quality management system possible that serves your business as second nature. This is certainly very feasible for all businesses. None of my customers who are "small businesses" have felt compelled to add more staff just by virtue of having an ISO-compliant quality management system. Another customer with just over a hundred staff added a QM professional to the team because he saw so much value in properly following the quality management system that they had written that that extra person actually increased their efficiency — that is a totally different ball game to believing that any quality management system will require more admin staff.

"I don't want to have to write down everything that we do, that will take for ever"

Most people are surprised when I tell them that ISO9001 has only six "mandatory documented procedures" i.e. there are only six areas where a documented procedure has to be part of a quality management system that satisfies the Standard's requirements. They are even more surprised when I add that you could probably cover all these six mandatory documented procedures on a couple of sides of A4. Yes it is true that there are many other areas of your operations that you actually would want to write down in some form but we are never looking at "War and Peace". You can document what you want to happen, or what your best practice should be, very simply with a few bullet points. Or via a simple step-by-step sequence. Or a diagram or a flow chart. Simplicity is the key. What will work for you? I always encourage my customers to think about leanness and efficiency right from the start. I have seen quality manuals that are six inches thick and are so off-putting that they never get used. They are just too daunting and sit on a shelf gathering dust. What use is that to any business? There is nothing in ISO that demands super-sophisticated explanations of a business's operations written in a prose that Jane Austen would approve. And if your operations take acres of newsprint to explain then maybe they need some simplification too.

And you don't have to write "everything" down either. Concentrate on your core activities, those that control your product and satisfy your customers. Depending on your company's culture, and every company has a culture whether it's thought about or not, some support activities may just happen or be second nature and don't need documenting in the early stages. The Standards are clear on what should be included in any management system so there is no need to go beyond that when you are just getting going.

"You need someone who loves paperwork; I'd never get my lot to do it"

Does anyone actually know "someone who loves paperwork"? I can't stand paperwork and form filling. But when I was contracting myself there was always a minimum of paperwork that helped control the job and that is what is important. For those people in your business who are key to your product but who "don't do paperwork" then the art is in devising, around them if necessary, that minimum of administration that keeps control and records key developments and completions. Even the most paperwork averse can be won over if you can demonstrate the role that record keeping and highlighting key milestones for example can play. I have had superb craftsmen in my teams who were never going to put pen to paper but they were so key that I put simple arrangements in place to get the essential minimum done by colleagues who didn't mind it. You never ever want paperwork for the sake of it and you need to be vigilant to make sure that does not happen. We had a rule that no piece of paper got into our system unless it clearly added to the control of our operations. Once it has passed that test then people are converted.

"None of us can write —articulate — a QM"

We're not talking Shakespeare here. We're talking about getting down what you actually do, or want to do, in delivering your product or service. You instinctively "know" what to do because of the practical skills and experience that encouraged you to start your business in the first place. The reality of serving and getting paid by customers also means that you "know" what needs to be done to keep customers happy. Any length of time in the construction industry, at whatever level, will have taught you, sometimes painfully, what situations you do and do not want to get yourself in. Getting all that down on paper, what you define as your best practice can be done as simply as you wish and we have mentioned bullet points, diagrams and flowcharts before. Whatever works. If you really struggle with getting it down and your business lacks someone who can do it then get outside help, just for the writing part. What you don't want to do, and there are some consultants who offer this, is buy in a quality management system written by someone else. The chances of that being totally relevant to you and your business are remote and therefore the chances of it being lean and efficient and guaranteed to serve your business are even slimmer. Your business is unique so your quality management system must be unique. It will come from the minds of you and your key people — guided of course by the tenets and requirements of ISO - that is the crucial bit. If you need help writing it down then so be it — that is the easy bit.

"We're too busy; I can't spare anyone for that"

As I said above, no one needs to be "spared" for ISO. The development of your quality management system should be integrated into your daily activities and, under the supervision of a good consultant should involve as many people as is practical. Various members of your staff looking after their area of expertise will bring rapid results without major detriment to the business.

And are you really too busy to develop a quality management system which will assure your customers, improve your business and manage your risks? Do you have all those three elements already in place to your satisfaction?

Chapter 11 — Geek Mythology

"The job is stressful enough without having to operate a quality management system"

Any Quality management system that adds stress to the job has completely missed the point. Or perhaps has been written by a consultant who is more concerned with the requirements of the Standards than the needs of the business. How does it go? "Fit ISO to your business; don't fit your business to ISO". Your management system should actually take the stress out of the job. Considered and practical explanation of what needs to be done, and/or what you want to be done, guides your staff as to what is required. Feeling stressed? Then take a look at the quality management system to see what happens next, to see what happens in certain situations, to see what your best practice is. Surely that will take the stress out, especially if, as it should be, your staff have both contributed to and fully understand how you do things. When confronted with problems and issues in the course of their activities your staff can consult the quality management system which even if it can't state exactly what to do next it can point them in the direction of a supervisor or manager i.e. can tell them where to get help, now.

Furthermore, you will be operating some form of "management system" whether you have thought about it or not. Often by default. If things are getting done there must be some system, informal or otherwise, operating. If it has not been devised along the lines of the internationally recognised standard for quality management then how you do know it is effective and is what the business needs? There is of course nothing wrong with informal systems if they work, absolutely not. But how can they assure a customer? How can they help a colleague who is looking for more guidance? They certainly cannot ensure that your best practice is employed on all occasions. Informality can lead to inconsistency and different interpretations of what is the right thing to do. If you have thought about what "Best Practice" means to you, and have enshrined it in your quality management system as a guide for all, then surely you have a greater chance of delivering consistent quality.

"It will take too long"

Too long when compared to what? How long is too long compared to continuing to operate inefficiently with overlap and underlap? Compared to not fully understanding the customer's requirements and issuing non-compliant tenders? Compared to consistently failing to get on approved tender lists because you cannot assure the potential customer that you have a demonstrable and effective quality management system? Compared to failing to get your high quality works handed over properly and doing them twice?

The process needn't take long anyway. And it needn't divert you and your key people away from essential day-to-day activities in running your business. In my experience developing a quality management system is best done in bite-size chunks, creating the building-blocks one-by-one in short intense bursts of activity. It needn't take anyone away from your business for days on end nor mean acres of time ring-fenced for ISO. Focused activity on desired elements of your quality management system in and amongst your routine business activities will make remarkable process. Most of my customers develop an integrated management system and achieve independent (see chapter on UKAS) Certification within a ten to twelve week period — perfectly feasible. One customer who had intense commercial pressure to secure Certification (as well as his desire to instil a management system with built-in improvement processes) started on November 21st and completed on December 20th. I wouldn't recommend that for everyone but it shows that it can be done. I will happily offer his name as a referee — he has agreed to do so — to anyone who wants to contact me.

Achieving ISO Certification is not and never should be a long drawn-out process. Taking too long militates against efficiency anyway. Once you start the process you need to generate some momentum to keep it flowing. Stop-start wastes so much time and energy in reviewing where you got up to last time before you can successfully push on. I also consider it very beneficial to impose a deadline. Deadlines are wonderful things and with commitment you will get there. The vast majority of my customers agree to set a deadline — of their own choosing — and we always meet it. The odd one or two that don't usually end up with a much more protracted and tortuous process.

"All the clause references confuse me"

Prefacing some valuable guidance or instructions with clause reference 4.2.1.3 and referring to clause reference 6.1.7.2 not only confuses people it can be very off-putting. I see so many QM's that use lots of clause references so that their manual mirrors the international Standards but in my experience, and so many people tell me this, it is an immediate turn off before the text — however great it is — is even looked at. Again this often comes from some consultant's slavish adherence to the Standards. You don't need clause references if you don't want them so leave them out. Some argue that you need them in so that an Auditor can easily assess your quality management system. Well call me old fashioned but it is not the purpose of your quality management system to make life easy for an Auditor — the purpose of your quality management system is to serve your business. Any good Auditor doesn't need clause references in your quality management system any way. You should organise your quality management system in the manner most appropriate to you and your business. It may follow the running order of the Standards but that it is not the deciding factor. What do you need to control your business and satisfy your customers? Once again, all together: "Fit ISO to your business ……." Okay, okay, I'm getting fed up with that as well but I'll only stop the chant if it has sunk in.

"Can't stand all the jargon"

Neither can I. Don't use it; I certainly avoid it whenever and wherever I can.

To be fair to the ISO people they are writing an international Standard and given the problems of translating into many languages it is perhaps inevitable that only some precise jargon can get the message across in all countries. But unless you're a multinational you don't need to worry about that so leave the jargon out. Of course there needs to be an understanding of what the jargon means, but trust me that can be achieved without too much hassle, but when it comes to developing your quality management system then do it in your business's everyday language that everyone understands. Just as with leaving out clause references, leaving out the jargon — expressing your quality management system in your everyday language — increases the accessibility of your quality management system and with that the chances of everybody buying in and using it to guide your business activities. Again, it has been argued to me that an Auditor will use the jargon when he comes along and it will be easier for him to do his job if he finds it in your quality management system. Well I refer you to my previous comments. Fit your business...

"Our customers are not asking for it"

Fair enough but there may come a time when they will. And even if they are not specifically asking for ISO Certification they will certainly appreciate improved performance that a well written quality management system will foster. You can never take satisfying your customers for granted and you can certainly never under-estimate the benefits of satisfying them even more. Improved performance can only strengthen your relationship with your customers. Beyond your customers asking for it there are the numerous other benefits of ISO to consider such as managing your risks and improving your bottom line which we have mentioned before.

Summary

Myths debunked:

- ISO will not cost a fortune
- It is not bureaucratic
- It is not inflexible
- It is for all businesses, large and small
- It is not all about the paperwork
- You will not need loads of training
- You will not need extra staff
- You don't need to write 'everything' down
- You don't need someone who loves paperwork
- Anyone can compile a Quality Manual
- It will reduce, not increase, stress
- You don't need to 'spare' anyone
- It is not a long drawn-out process
- You don't need jargon!

12

What Not To Do

For me the number one sin in seeking to secure ISO Certification is to "impose" the Standard on to your business or buy-in a Standard-compliant Quality Management System and decide that is now how you are going to do things. That is trying to fit your business to ISO, not fitting ISO to your business. I don't think there is anything more guaranteed to breed resentment, frustration and resistance. I always remember a fantastic phrase I learnt on a Dale Carnegie course many years ago, "People support a world they help to create". I think the opposite is also true, people find it hard to support a world imposed upon them.

If any Standard is applied blindly, clause by clause, jargon by jargon, then it is going to struggle to get buy-in from the troops charged with working it. Who wants to have to do their jobs slavishly following an imposed set of instructions?

I see so many so-called Quality Management Systems that are nothing more than a rehash of the Standard with a nod here and there to what the business actually does. Actually sometimes you would not even know what the business does because their "quality management system" really is just a

Chapter 12 — What Not To Do

document that is a version of the relevant Standard with their business name added here and there.

Or even if there is the occasional mention of the business and its personnel you get no feel for the culture of the business or its unique attributes. I was once asked to look over the putative Quality Management System of a leading subcontractor in his field and found a System that would have scored 100% for blind allegiance to the Standard but zero in terms of reflecting the excellence of a leading subcontractor or the personality of a dynamic young MD who was already forging a name for himself in his field. Had that system been adopted - I still think imposed is a better word - it would have acted as a break on the business not the platform for it to go from strength to strength. All this gives ISO a bad name. Letter of the law rather than spirit of the law.

Chapter 12 — What Not To Do

The Standard does not have to be applied either unquestioningly clause by clause nor in the order that the clauses appear in the Standard. As we have seen, you don't even need to adopt the clause references either and for most businesses why would you? A firm of solicitors might feel very comfortable with "clause 4.2.3.1" and "see clause 5.6.1.4" but why should a firm of plasterers, or electricians? In my experience this is such a turn-off for most people. Of course you need some referencing and sequencing but ease of use is the motivation. What's more, when you get sucked into the tyranny of clause references you find yourself inventing some burdensome procedure for each one.

All the above results from the approach of starting with the Standards first. I hear horror stories of consultants walking in with files and files of "notes" about what ISO demands and telling the business that this is what you have to do. Or even worse, they walk in with a standard Quality Management System solution which they are "selling". A one-size-fits-all approach. You might as well buy something similar off the internet and cut and paste your name into it for all the good that it will do you.

I am sometimes asked to help customers who "have 9001" but "nobody uses it anymore". I pretty much know what to expect before I even arrive at the customer's offices. I meet the MD or some other member of Top Management and am given the dreaded file; you guessed it, about six inches thick. My heart sinks. Clearly an unread document, the Quality Management System is in pristine condition as it has not been overburdened with use. And lo and behold, here we go. Beautifully bound, lovely colours, nice font...and bearing no relation whatsoever to the business in question.

Chapter 12 — What Not To Do

The first and last place the business name appears is on the front cover – and usually the consultant's name appears on every page. Unimaginative lip service to the Standard, line by boring line, drowning in jargon. More imagination applied to a labyrinthine bureaucracy than to the needs of the business. Wonderfully complex forms to be filled in that tick boxes rather than serve the business and its operations. The idea of "effectiveness" does not seem to have entered the process. When I get asked what is to be done with it I promise you I am as polite as possible and try and think of the nicest way to say "Bin it!" There is nothing to be done with a "Quality Management System" like that except start again.

On another occasion, an ex-subcontractor of mine, a really competent subcontractor who was one of my safest pairs of hands, asked me once I had started Foy Certification if I could help them "add 14001 and 18001 to their existing ISO 9001 System". They were expanding and wanted to work for some main contractors who quite rightly insisted that they were certified to the three

Chapter 12 – What Not To Do

Standards. Of course I was delighted at the prospect of helping a former subbie but I hadn't realised that they already had 9001. When I questioned him about that he said he had only just realised himself, the new owner had just told him, yet he'd been running operations, well I hasten to add, for a few years. I was immediately suspicious, and concerned from a friendly point of view, and asked to see his ISO Certificate and his Quality Management System. The certificate broke all the rules of UKAS (United Kingdom Accreditation Services, see chapter 13) and I will come back to this story for a different reason than the one that concerns us now. When I saw his Quality Management System it was as I described above. Undoubtedly faithful to the Standard, but not recognisable in any way as a document that my friend's business used on a regular basis, or God forbid, actually contributed to the business and its effectiveness. Moreover, my friend had been running his activities blissfully unaware of its existence! So what was it there for? Who had contributed to it? What business need did it serve? It transpired that it had been "bought in" by a previous owner, imposed without troubling the concepts of relevance, appropriateness, and efficacy, had added nothing, and then sat vegetating ever since. A prime example of what not to do when developing a Quality Management System. There is another very serious down side to this particular story which we'll come to later.

I would also advise against engaging a consultant on open-ended day rates. As an ex-contractor myself I never liked "Daywork". I charge a fixed fee for consultancy to develop an Integrated Management System and sometimes this has worked very well for me and sometimes it hasn't but I still think it is the right thing to do. More controversially, I would advise that you engage a consultant with extensive experience of the construction industry. Your man, or lady, needs to be a construction person as much as an ISO Consultant. He or she needs to know instinctively the nature of the environment that you operate in, the challenges you face on a daily basis, the reality of being a construction subcontractor. If the opposite is true, you may have a superbly knowledgeable ISO man but he either has to spend lots of time understanding the reality of

Chapter 12 — What Not To Do

the construction industry or he may be offering management system solutions that will be ISO-compliant but not necessarily the best way forward for your business. The vast majority of my customers are construction subcontractors. I have however been referred to businesses outside construction and have occasionally agreed to help them. I have helped to secure Certification for example for a medical software business and a mobile app developer. Inevitably, there had to be time spent on understanding their respective businesses and I was still learning through the whole process. They were successfully certified and I was delighted that the Standards proved so comprehensive in their coverage that highly effective Integrated Management Systems were created. My point is that I couldn't walk through the door and instinctively know what the business was about and get straight on with it.

Arguably the biggest single reason for businesses to fail to secure Certification, or to get it and not keep it, is the failure of Top Management to be fully involved. Leadership is one of the Eight Quality Management Principles and for the ISO Standards the involvement of Top Management is inescapable. I have heard stories of Auditors visiting business for the first time to be met by the "Quality Manager" or even the MD's PA and it becoming clear very quickly that the Directors have never been anywhere near the shiny new manual eagerly anticipating its assessment. Any true Auditor will get his coat and politely leave. It is your business and ISO Certification will make it better, so why would you not want to be in it up to your neck? Announce you decision to seek Certification, trumpet it. Tell them why. Lead by example and you will be surprised at the positive reaction from your team.

Involvement of people is also, as we have seen, one of the Eight Quality Management Principles. I would argue that you want as many people as is practically possible inputting to your developing System. Even if you as the MD or owner are fully committed in principle, you certainly do not want to give it to a member of staff "as a project". While this is at least unfair to the individual

Chapter 12 — What Not To Do

involved, it is hardly likely to result in your best System. The last thing you want is for your System to be associated with one person. It then becomes "Bill's system" or the "FD's system" and that is dangerous in terms of eventually getting buy-in. It can certainly be led by one person, and the more senior the better, but you want serious and considered contributions as to what your best practice should be. More people than you might initially imagine are itching to have their say, not least to make their area more efficient and effective but also to influence communication channels to them and from them.

Guard against overly complex processes. That makes them harder to execute and with too many points at which they can fall down. It also makes it so much harder at audit time of course. Keep it simple. Accept also that you will not get this perfectly right first time. Your System can be good enough to secure ISO Certification but will still naturally evolve through use. In fact it is only through continued use and the continued challenge of customers and events that your System gets honed. Twelve months after Certification your system will be different, sometimes very different!

You do not of course ever want paperwork for the sake of it; my rule was always that no piece of paper ever got into our Integrated Management System unless it unequivocally demonstrated that it made control of our projects easier.

Don't think that you can develop an Integrated Management System in bits and pieces fitting it in whenever and wherever you can during occasional breaks in your hectic schedule. While, as I have said elsewhere, the process will not take you or anybody else "out of your business" for long periods it does need time being allocated for it to be successful. Not as much as you might think and I talk about this later.

A very important part of any Integrated Management System is guidance on what to do if things go wrong, as they inevitably will from time to time. You

Chapter 12 — What Not To Do

will have arrangements in place to deal with such situations. A very common problem I see in the early days of implementation is people jumping on every little thing that doesn't go to plan and flagging it up as an issue to be investigated and put right. You have to be very specific here about what you consider to be a "problem". ISO expects you to investigate major problems, get to the root cause and put them right so they don't happen again. Quite right too. It is madness to keep making the same mistakes as I'm sure you will agree. But you have to be clear about what "problems" or instances this reaction relates to. If you erect a one-hour fire-rated partition when it should have been a two-hour fire-rated partition then that is clearly something that has to be investigated and made sure it never happens again. There are some issues however where a manager just deals with things. If the wrong box of screws turns up I don't think you really want to be launching an investigation, your site manager will just sort it out (if the wrong box of screws turns up every time then that is different). I see some great systems absolutely hamstrung by too many people recording every little thing that goes wrong and raising the "non-conformance" flag. Files and files accumulate, they can never all be "investigated" and the whole process falls into disrepute. Be sensible about what you class as "non-conformity" and limit it to serious issues that you definitely would not want to happen again.

Some businesses as we have seen want ISO Certification just to get onto a tender list or because of pressure from a customer. It would be a shame however if any business going to the effort of securing Certification did not then go on to enjoy all the benefits that a properly developed and implemented Integrated Management System can convey. Moreover, they will have to devote time and effort to keeping their Certification even if they had just paid lip service to the process to get on that tender list. I know a few companies who have ISO Certification purely to satisfy external pressures and don't fully use their System in their everyday business. What happens here is that sooner or later audit time rolls around. The business goes into panic mode because "the Auditor is coming"! For a week or so the place is in turmoil, everyone like teenagers cramming for an exam. At what cost to the business I shudder to think. If ISO Certification is retained they then put their system back into mothballs until the next audit visit. Don't do this, this is crazy. Why spend so much time keeping ISO Certification for a System you don't get the benefit of? Use your System, live it, challenge it, improve it. Improve your business at the same time. When you do that an Auditor could walk through the door unannounced at any time and it will hold no fears.

Chapter 12 — Summary

Summary

What not to do:

- Impose a system
- Leave Top Management out of it
- Buy-in a standard solution
- Engage a Consultant on Open-ended day rates
- Do it just for the tick in a box
- Beat yourself up with non-conformities

13

The Only Way Is UKAS

I qualified as a Lead Auditor for ISO 9001, ISO 14001 and OHSAS 18001 but I don't want to do any auditing. I wanted the qualifications so that I understood what the Auditors were looking for and how they went about ISO audits and also so that I could represent my customers when it came to **their** audits. Because there is a certain amount of discretion applying ISO Standards, because I believe you should apply them in the leanest, most practical and efficient manner possible, and because you know I believe that you should do so in a manner entirely appropriate to your business, I anticipated that there might be occasions when I might need to defend what my customers — with my encouragement — did within their Management Systems. Indeed, there have been a few instances when that has been the case and a debate, always friendly and professional I hasten to add, has ensued on the proposed solution to an ISO Requirement. I would like to paraphrase Brian Clough (showing my age there), and say that the debate continues until all parties agree I am right. Not quite, but there has only been one occasion when an Auditor and I have had to agree to disagree and to be honest the point in question was so technical that the customer wondered what we were both going on about! Overall this has never really been a problem but I

Chapter 13 — The Only Way Is UKAS

am glad I am able to look an Auditor in the eye. And I do think the combination of practical experience of implementing the Standards when I was a contractor and the qualification of auditing is a strong one for my customers.

I occasionally get asked why I don't do auditing as well as consultancy and the answer is simple. There has to be a distinct independence between consulting and auditing. I could consult for you or I could audit for you; I absolutely could not do both. You cannot be poacher **and** gamekeeper. The principle of independence is fundamental to the whole business and so fixed in my mind as to be beyond discussion. There **are** businesses who will do both, who will assist you to develop a Quality Management System and then will audit it. Now, wouldn't you always pass an audit if the fellow who helped you develop your System was the same fellow who was now testing it? Maybe that is me being cynical. Of course an organisation offering both services might have Fred doing the consulting and Bill doing the auditing but how strictly independent can they be if they are working for the same organisation? This is not casting any aspersions against Fred or Bill. Fred could be the best consultant around and there is absolutely nothing to say that the System he helps to develop is not ISO compliant and also effective for the business. Bill may be a superb, robust no-stone-left-unturned Auditor who – unlike me perhaps – has the ability to remain totally objective and there is no reason why his auditing is not as thorough as anybody else's and therefore his recommendation can be relied upon. Still doesn't seem right to me that the same organisation is doing both. Who's keeping Fred on his toes? Bill? Well who's keeping Bill on his toes?

It is of course not important what seems right or wrong to me. What would your customers think of this arrangement? The very people who are looking to your Certification to assure them that you are a safe pair of hands. One or two of my customers have actually said to me, "Can't you audit us?" Well yes I can and I have the qualifications to do so. But what would an "Andrew Foy Certificate of ISO Compliance" actually mean to you? And most importantly, mean to your

Chapter 13 – The Only Way Is UKAS

customer? I would be very flattered if you trusted me enough to not only help you develop an ISO-compliant Integrated Management System but then also accepted my assurance, via my (!) audit, that it was sound in every respect and that you should now go and tell the world. Wouldn't your customers say, "Well who is Andrew Foy?"

By contrast, what if you were audited by an Auditor from a firm of professional Auditors (a Certification Body) who is not only independent of me and can have no professional connection to me, but who has also had to jump through hoops to have the privilege of, and the accreditation for, auditing you, and is furthermore under as much scrutiny at audit time as you are, and is assessed himself in the very process of assessing you? Would any resulting Certification from a body like that not be immensely more valuable to your customer than the Andrew Foy version? If there was also a government sponsored agency that "accredited" such Certification Bodies and published those who qualify on a list on the internet for the whole world to see, wouldn't that be even more reassuring?

That arrangement exists in the UK. The United Kingdom Accreditation Service (UKAS) **accredits** Certification Bodies (Auditors) who then go on to audit and **certify** your business. As the national Accreditation Body, UKAS is the only body recognised by Government to assess Auditors against internationally recognised Standards, thereby determining in the public interest their technical competence and integrity. Accredited organisations are entitled to display symbols that incorporate the Royal Crown, signifying Government recognition of the accreditation process.

When we discussed PAS2030 we discovered that The Department for Energy and Climate Change (DECC) has appointed UKAS to accredit Auditors for the Certification of Green Deal advisors and installers. With regards to the Green Deal, as with ISO, this is to provide consumers with confidence that there is a "chain of competence" right through to those installing the energy efficient measures.

Chapter 13 — The Only Way Is UKAS

So accreditation is designed to establish that the Auditor is impartial, technically competent and meets the required performance standard. This is a bit different to the world of Fred and Bill above. Why would you go to the effort of developing an Integrated Management System and then leave the Certification of it to chance? Wouldn't you want the UKAS (www.ukas.com) symbol on your paperwork, with its national and international recognition? Doesn't your PQQ ask if you have ISO Certification from a UKAS-accredited body? This is certainly becoming an increasing stipulation in the public sector and will help you to win more business. Only UKAS-approved Certification would allow you to be entered on the UK Register of Quality Assessed Companies.

Chapter 13 — The Only Way Is UKAS

Certification issued by an organisation not accredited by UKAS (Bill!) could well lead to it not being recognised by a customer whom you want to work for. Do you remember my friend who discovered that the business he worked for had bought in a compliant management system and had then had it "audited" by the same organisation they bought the system off? When he was in an important meeting with a potential new customer the new owner of that business was almost laughed out of the office when he produced, unknowingly, his non UKAS-accredited 9001 certificate. Don't let this happen to you. A non-accredited certificate cannot give your customers confidence in your management system, it simply does not have the same credibility as a certificate underlined by a third party Accreditation Body such as UKAS. The Department of Energy and Climate Change (DECC) has appointed UKAS to accredit Auditors for the Certification of Green Deal advisors and installers. With regards to the Green Deal, as with ISO, this is to provide consumers with confidence that there is a "chain of competence" right through to those installing the energy efficient measures.

Chapter 13 — Summary

Summary

Get certified by an independent UKAS accredited Auditor:

- Always.
- Period.
- No exceptions.
- End of.
- No more, no less.

14

The 8 Step Methodology

In gaining a 100% success rate of securing ISO Certification (in the vast majority of cases Triple Certification to 9001/14001/18001 via an integrated Management System) I have developed the following proven methodology for not only passing your audits but also maximising the benefits of developing an Integrated Management System i.e. going beyond Certification to realise true long-term ongoing value.

Step 1: Preliminary

Understand the business needs and why it is considering ISO and what it hopes to get from securing Certification.

Step 2: Visualisation

With that understanding, "Begin with the End" in Mind (thank you Stephen Covey, the first of your 7 Habits of Highly Successful People) visualising the ideal management system incorporating more than just the Requirements of ISO.

Step 3: Analysis

Compare current arrangements with the ideal visualised and also the Requirements of an Integrated Management System certifiable to ISO 9001, ISO 14001, and OHSAS 18001 (and indeed PAS if required).

Step 4: Planning and Deadline

A successful analysis step will allow us to gauge how much time and effort will be involved in developing an Integrated Management System. With that knowledge we can plan the workload and, crucially, set a deadline (for the Stage 1 Audit at the very least.

Step 5: Construction

Build your System and enshrine your best practice. Get buy-in, look each other in the eye and commit. Lead by example.

Step 6: Stage 1 Audit

Review your System for conformance and pass your Stage 1 Audit first time.

Step 7: Stage 2 Audit

Execute the compulsory improvement activities between the Stages and pass your Stage 2 Audit first time.

Step 8: Continual Improvement

Embrace the Standards, live your Integrated Management System and improve your business, continually!

Chapter 14 — The 8 Step Methodology

Business Growth through Quality Assurance

Post-Certification
- 8 Continual Improvement Step
- 7 Pass Stage 2

Certification
- 6 Pass Stage 1
- 5

Pre-Certification
- Construction Step
- 4 Planning & Deadline Step
- 3 Analysis Step
- 2 Visualisation Step
- 1 Preliminary Step

Business Improvement
Customer Assurance
Open up New Markets

Your Best Practice
Risk Management

ONGOING — Fit ISO to your business; don't expect your business to fit to ISO
Embrace the Standards and build long-term value into your business

2-3 WEEKS — First time execution of Improvement Processes and pass Stage 2 Audit first time

Review and Approve and pass the Stage 1 Audit first time

6-8 WEEKS — Build your system from the bottom up; enshrining Best Practice

INITIAL CONSULTATION — Understand and plan - with a deadline - the workload involved

Where are you now in relation to where you want to be?

PRE-CONSULTATION — What does your ideal Integrated Management System look like?

Why do you want/need ISO Certification?

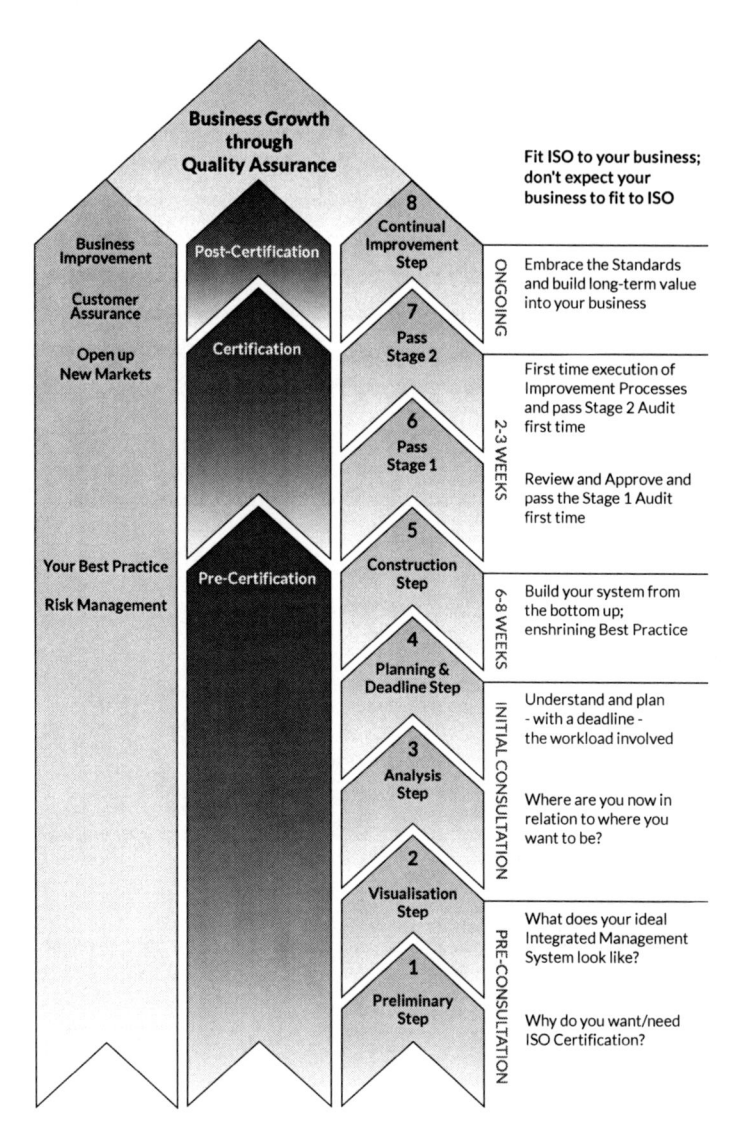

Our 8-Step ISO Success Methodology

Chapter 14 — The 8 Step Methodology

Step 1: Preliminary

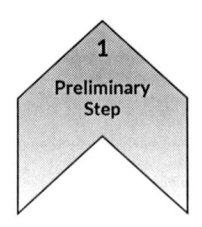

There are lots of reasons why businesses want to secure ISO Certification. We talked earlier about internal and external motivation, about the benefits and will discuss in detail business improvement in chapter 15. We have also already made the point that the decision to develop an ISO 9001-compliant Quality Management System or an Integrated Management System and secure independent Certification should be a strategic one. It **should** change your business for the better and **will** do so if implemented properly.

Before you commence the process you should step back and ask yourself some key questions:

- What do you want for your business?

- What would it ideally look like?

- What would you want customers to think about it?

- What would your culture feel like, how would you want your employees to feel?

- What do you consider best practice in delivering your product or service?

- Why are you considering ISO Certification?

- Is there an external or internal motivation, or ideally both?

Chapter 14 — The 8 Step Methodology

Developing your integrated management system should take all these issues into account.

ISO can offer a positive dimension to all these considerations. I have argued above that it is wrong to start with a view to imposing ISO on your business; surely the starting point is to decide what the business needs and see how ISO helps that. This is where my cliché of fitting ISO to your business not expecting it to fit to ISO comes from. As we saw earlier it is a common reason, and a legitimate one initially to come to ISO from some external pressure such as the need to work for a particular customer or in a particular business sector. But the title of this book is "Not Just a Tick In A Box" and surely you want to gain all the benefits of ISO and not just be able to tick the box that says "Is your business Certified to ISO 9001?" on your desired customers' PQQ. It is going to take some effort (not as much as you might think and perfectly feasible for most businesses) to be able to put that tick in the box, especially if your customer demands quite rightly that you are independently certified by a UKAS-accredited Certification Body — and you can bet your life that any decent customer will make that demand — then why not embrace the process and enjoy all the benefits of ISO Certification and build in to your business those improvement activities that generate long-term value.

So the first things I want to understand at the first meeting with my customer are why he is thinking about ISO and what does his business need. I'm not walking in with a copy of the Standards under one arm and a ready-made "Andrew Foy standard solution" under the other. The answers to these initial questions if fully explored will inform the whole process and result in my customer's tailor-made solution of infinitely more value. This first step does not take long at all, it really can be a quick chat, but is very important. If he is initially motivated by the desire to get on a particular tender list then I consider it my duty to inform him of all the other benefits of ISO Certification. Of course there are common elements to any ISO solution, as we have seen, for the very reason that these common elements or Requirements have been identified by great minds as being essential to any Integrated Management System. The requirements may be common; the solution to satisfying those requirements should be anything but.

Step 2: Visualisation

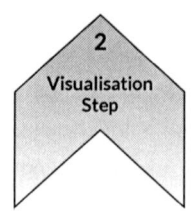

I urge you the customer to look beyond ISO Certification to what you want your System to be; there is no reason why it cannot be an all-embracing management system that effectively controls your operations but also a marketing document, an induction tool and a training document. It can and should show your business in its best light.

I want to know what the business currently does well - in its own view and its customers' view – and what it can do better. You may have already answered this question by deciding that your delivery is inconsistent and/or you have trouble handing projects over suggesting some deficiency in you quality assurance or Handover procedures. You may be concerned about Health & Safety risks or environmental worries and want to tighten those areas up. Knowing your priorities in particular can allow us to focus the effort of developing a compliant Integrated Management System in general.

It is also important to know if there are any other stipulations the business works under. For examples codes of practice from a particular trade association or the likes of NICEIC as my electrical contractor customers do. These additional requirements should be built into the management system in order to give the business a one-stop solution to managing its activities.

Chapter 14 — The 8 Step Methodology

Finally I want to know about what is unique about your business. What are its USP's? What is its particular culture that you want to reflect in your Quality Management System because that is certainly possible and should be attempted? What are you as the MD particularly proud of and want to shout about? Why would you not want to enshrine all this within your Integrated Management System? We are not aiming at that six inch document which has been thrust into my hands so many times. Your lean, practical, efficient Management System, which is what should be aimed for, can also be a superb marketing document that says everything about you. So get it all in there. You work hard to differentiate yourself so make sure your Management System promotes this.

Isn't all this a world away from the approach of pouring over every word of the Standard and telling you what you have to do to "get 9001" or whatever? And don't you think the resulting document - if this approach is adopted - will be a world away from the lonely behemoth sat neglected on a shelf? Furthermore, the corollary of course to deciding all the good stuff you want in, is to decide what you definitely don't want in. I think running a business is sometimes like driving over many years. We all acquire bad habits along the way which militate against best practice. Over the years, businesses evolve ways of doing things some good some bad; inefficient and wasteful practices can creep in. "That's just the way we do things," gains currency. When you decide to develop an Integrated Management System don't miss the opportunity to rationalise what you do, get rid of the less effective stuff, for example those bits of paperwork that were generated for one particular instance and have somehow hung around. Take the opportunity to drop the baggage. Again, this need not be a long process and a good idea of what you want can be acquired very quickly. And of course your ideal System is likely to evolve during the whole process anyway so we are just looking for a general direction here.

Step 3: Analysis

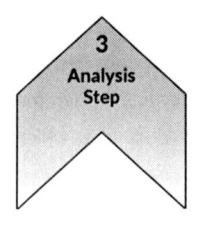

With a commitment to developing the best Quality Management System we can, with an understanding of why we are doing this, and with an understanding of what the business needs let's get down to the nitty gritty. Whilst our motivation for developing a Quality Management System is definitely Not Just a tick in a Box it is actually worth looking at how many boxes we are actually ticking in the first place. By this I mean looking at how many Requirements of the Standards your business is currently satisfying, often without realising it. Any business doing well or indeed even just surviving in the recent brutality of the construction industry must be doing something right. At this stage I walk through with my customers the Requirements of an Integrated Management System as far as ISO is concerned and show where the other elements we have already decided that we want included in our own unique bespoke System should fit. Most of my customers are pleasantly surprised with how many Requirements they are already satisfying and this gives a boost to the rest of the process. You will have gathered by now that I don't particularly like jargon but this process is often referred to as a gap analysis i.e. determine the gaps between where you want to be and where you are now to get a definitive solution.

This step usually takes no more than a few hours and the process allows us to gauge pretty accurately what the extent of the workload is in developing a compliant Quality Management System and, depending on the level of commitment, the timescale also. We are usually left with a mixture of new items to be developed and others to be enhanced or honed to satisfy where we want to be. For both situations, and the Standards and the Quality Management Principles which we have discussed at length are our guiding lights here, the motivation has to be the opportunity to enshrine best practice as you would want it to be in your business. You might already have a very clear idea of what

Chapter 14 — The 8 Step Methodology

you want. If not the principles and the Standards can guide the way. By the way, when I have walked through my Integrated Management System template with customers, which contain all the Requirements of ISO 9001, ISO14001 and OHSAS 18001, nobody has ever said to me "why would you do that" in relation to any particular Requirement. That reinforces my view that the Standards are superbly well written and have effective practical application for all construction specialists.

Often when businesses who have not really thought about how they want to do things and what best practice would be have just got on with attracting their first customers, have started well and got repeat business. Before they know it they have become successful and events have taken over. People are working under pressure, corners are cut and the response is reactive rather than proactive. And that becomes the norm. Work is getting done but maybe in not the most efficient and cost-effective way. Is your business like that? What are those methods and procedures you have always wanted to instil but have never had the chance to do so because you have been in the trenches for so long?

Step 4: Planning and Deadline

If you are developing a Quality Management System then now is the time to decide exactly how you want things to happen. And this is where I encourage my customers to enlist as much input as possible from key members of staff. The best person to decide the most effective way of estimating should be your Lead Estimator. Control of your operations on site should be largely influenced by your best Site Manager and so on. You might have witnessed best practice that you really appreciated or were impressed with by another contractor and you want to do something similar. Maybe your customers are demanding a certain way of doing things. Well now is the time to address all those opportunities and get them into your Quality

Chapter 14 — The 8 Step Methodology

Management System. Of course, the more people you involve the more likely you are to get buy-in from your key staff. I'm certainly not advocating decision by committee but you want the insights of your specialists. I was always very pleasingly surprised when some great ideas came from our sites for example. What we have already decided that you do well may go straight into your Quality Management System or do so with a little tweak here and there. Develop your project plan based on your gap analysis and decide how much or how little documentation you need to demonstrate control. Clearly you might need a consultant here.

To structure your Management System your watch-words are simplicity and user-friendliness. You are not seeking sophistication, certainly not at this stage. Ease of use, practicality, efficiency and effectiveness are what you are aiming for, especially when encouraging input from your key people. Always remember the simple Process Approach that is at the heart of ISO i.e. Plan-Do-Check & Act. I'll remind you of the way I look at this: I see Planning as what you need to do to prepare your business to enter the market and engage with customers. We have seen when we looked at the Requirements of the Standards that this means planning what processes you require to determine your customer's requirements and deliver your product or service accordingly from a Quality point of view; and from an Environmental and Health & Safety point of view it means, amongst other things, understanding your environmental aspects and impacts and health & safety risks respectively. You will need controls to manage your impacts and your risks and you will need a mechanism, as we have seen, to understand, comply with and keep up to date with the legal framework.

The Doing is your implementation and operation of your planned processes. Here you will want to control your activities so that they conform to your plans and ensure that your product or service is consistently delivered in a manner you have determined to be your business' best practice.

Chapter 14 — The 8 Step Methodology

Checking and Acting is the monitoring, review and, most importantly, the improvement of your processes to the benefit of your business. Obviously you need to have an eye on the Standards when developing all this to ensure that you satisfy the Requirements of each. Your consultant's job is to ensure that you satisfy the Requirements first and foremost but equally important that, you guessed it, you fit ISO to your business and don't go about fitting your business to ISO. It is absolutely vital also that it is your Management System and not your consultants' and is certainly not a clone of the Standards with your name copied and pasted here and there. It must be in your everyday language that your business uses and encapsulate your culture. Involving your people (one of the Eight Quality Management Principles remember) in the development of your System will ensure that they are keen to use it, make it work, and improve it. My approach is to let the business build the System in the manner they want to do things, explaining which of the Requirements they are satisfying as they do so and obviously raising any Requirements that are not automatically getting satisfied in the process. These would have been identified in the gap analysis anyway and are then added in, again in the manner most appropriate to the business, at logical points within the overall System.

I think it is crucial to set a deadline, at least for the ISO Stage 1 Audit. By that I mean getting the Stage 1 Audit booked with a Certification Body and "in the diary". A thorough analysis will allow us to make a thorough plan. With that in mind there is no reason why we cannot set that deadline. Most of my customers have set a deadline and guess what, we have always made it to the Stage 1 Audit and what's more we have always passed. The shortest time from the Preliminary Step to the Stage 2 Audit Step, i.e. Triple Certification from scratch, in my experience is four weeks. My customer simply had to have his Certification in that period to satisfy a contractual obligation in regard to some large projects he had won. I wouldn't recommend that timescale but it shows that it can be done. The average time taken by my customers from start to Stage 1 Audit is six weeks to eight weeks; with a further average two or

Chapter 14 — The 8 Step Methodology

three weeks between Stages 1 and 2. That gives an overall timescale of eight to ten or eleven weeks for the whole process. This is certainly feasible by any business serious about getting certified. We will look closer at the effort involved when we consider the next step but it's worth saying here that this timescale never involves you or any of your staff being taken away from your business needs for long periods.

A deadline not only gives you a target it compels momentum. If you don't have momentum and pick up the process haphazardly you spend so much time recapping where you have got to and revisiting your plan again and again to try and get moving. This wastes so much time. It's fatal to think that you can do this "when we're not busy". When are you ever "not busy"? For the handful of my customers who have not set a deadline the process has been tortuous. One small business took twelve months and one, admittedly larger business, took fifteen months (both had decided that they wanted to "see how things go" and maybe set a deadline further down the line). That of course was not twelve months or fifteen months of continuous activity. Far from it, it was a snatched few hours here and a few there in between "busy" periods. In fact, the only reason the process was ever completed was because at some point everyone got so fed up that we – yes, you got it – **decided to set a deadline**! Once the Rubicon was crossed both businesses successfully secured Certification in a matter of weeks.

Once you have decided to go for ISO Certification, announce it to your business immediately. Tell everyone why you are doing this and what you expect to get from it. Tell all your staff that you certainly expect cooperation but, more than that, you welcome active participation in the process.

Step 5: Construction

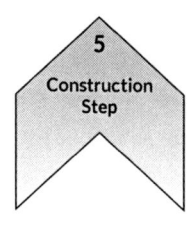

We now know why we are doing this, where we want to be, what we have to do, and when we have to do it by. So we can set about building your System from the bottom up, deciding what is best practice for you. We are going to keep and enshrine what you do well and add those ISO elements which hitherto we have not been doing.

In deciding your best practice you are not only trying to enhance the quality of your delivery but also ensure the consistency of your delivery. This is the best way you can see of delivering your product or service and this is how you want it done again and again; so that your business becomes synonymous with quality performance. There are two important points to make and bear in mind both of which we will discuss in more detail later on. Although I will always urge you to consider and take on board the Quality Management Principles and of course the actual Standards in deciding your best practice – we are of course on one level attempting to satisfy a set of Requirements – your solutions have to be, as emphasised earlier, appropriate to your business. The other very important points are that although you are deciding on your best practice you are never saying anything that is cast in stone. Remember that continual improvement is a fundamental ISO Principle and surely one of the most important motivating factors in seeking ISO Certification in the first place. You should be very definite about how you want things done but simultaneously open to being challenged by the suggestion of doing it even better. We will look at this in chapter 15. You will not create the perfect Integrated Management System first time. It is very important to realise that not only is this impossible first time around but is not required of you. Yes, we have to satisfy the Requirements of the Standards but we should aim to do so at a minimum level at first. It is perfectly legitimate to satisfy an ISO Requirement at our first attempt at Certification knowing

Chapter 14 — The 8 Step Methodology

that we can do better in time. This is why the reasonably quick timescales I outlined above are possible. You can define your process for satisfying a particular Requirement with a compliant solution for Audit time and with a plan to improve it over a period after Certification. This plan to improve would obviously sit in your "Objectives and Targets" box, thereby also satisfying another Requirement!

You will know from earlier chapters on the individual requirements of the Standards that as a minimum we need:

- Policy statements

- An organisation chart with defined roles and responsibilities

- A "Management Representative" or a custodian of the system

- Plans for quality delivery of our product and service

- An understanding of our environmental impact and our health and safety risks and the legalities around both

- Objectives and Targets

- Operational procedures

- The six Mandatory Procedures we talked about earlier

- Arrangements for training and ensuring competence

- Monitoring and review procedures, some of which are prescribed by ISO and some will be unique to you.

Chapter 14 – The 8 Step Methodology

This last item is obviously about improvement (Check and Act) and we will look at this in detail in chapter 15.

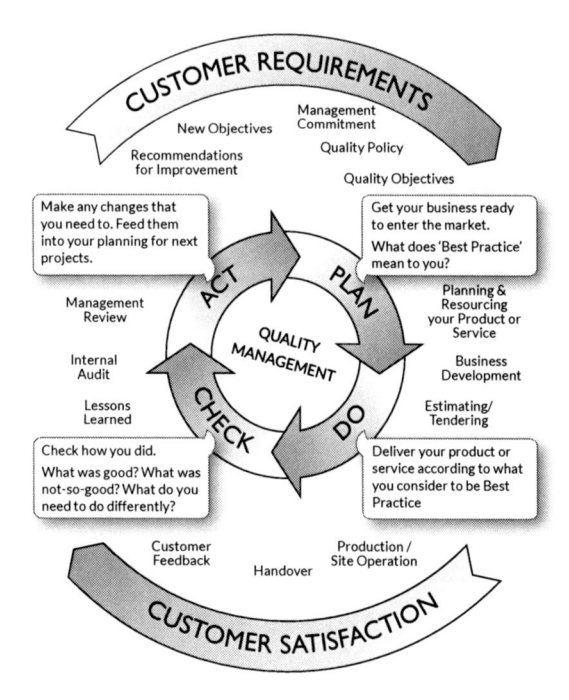

CUSTOMER REQUIREMENTS

- Management Commitment
- New Objectives
- Quality Policy
- Recommendations for Improvement
- Quality Objectives

PLAN: Get your business ready to enter the market. What does 'Best Practice' mean to you?
- Planning & Resourcing your Product or Service
- Business Development
- Estimating/Tendering

DO: Deliver your product or service according to what you consider to be Best Practice
- Production / Site Operation
- Handover
- Customer Feedback

CHECK: Check how you did. What was good? What was not-so-good? What do you need to do differently?
- Lessons Learned
- Internal Audit
- Management Review

ACT: Make any changes that you need to. Feed them into your planning for next projects.

QUALITY MANAGEMENT

CUSTOMER SATISFACTION

Plan-Do-Check & Act and ISO Requirements

Think about your Policy Statements – Quality, Environmental, and Health & Safety – as being key documents that say everything you want to be and do in these areas. You certainly have to make some clear ISO commitments in your Policy Statements but they can also be used to declare the type of company you want to be and can guide the rest of the process. Written well they can be very motivating for your people and point your business to your Vision as well as being consistent with what you know your customers want from you.

Chapter 14 — The 8 Step Methodology

Policy Statements should be the driving force of your business and state your commitment to satisfying the Standards and improving your business. They are also of course one of the first items that any Auditor will look at.

The Policy Statements, which of course must be reviewed periodically, are also a great place to declare your objectives for the forthcoming period. Failure to adequately define your Quality Policy, for example, and subsequently your Quality Objectives will raise major problems in successfully implementing the Standards. While your improvement objectives can include anything you wish, ISO will expect to see objectives that improve the way your product or service consistently meets customer requirements, that increase the effectiveness of your processes and procedures, and thereby positively influence the way your customers perceive you. I haven't said this for a long time but you can't argue with that can you?

As you build your Integrated Management System you not only need to think about individual processes but also their interaction, especially across functions. Lots of construction specialists hit problems for example when a successful tender is handed over to the site team. You need to think about your whole process from receiving an enquiry to handing over a successful installation to your customer. How do your various functions relate to each other successfully so nothing falls between two stools? Hence the Quality Management Principle, a System Approach to Management.

As we said earlier, nowhere do the Standards say that you need an intricate, detailed set of documentation to do this. Bullet points, diagrams, flow charts, and a combination of all three – whatever works for you and the simpler the better. The level of detail is to be determined by you to ensure effectiveness. You do want your manual to guide your staff as to best practice and what to do in certain situations but there will be areas where you can rely on their skills and

Chapter 14 — The 8 Step Methodology

experience as well. There will be other areas where you have bought in some software that does the job for you, for example estimating packages. This can be referred to in your System and you just need to make sure that adequate training is provided to ensure the competence to use the software.

DO YOU DO WHAT YOU SAY YOU DO

We said earlier that this process should not divert you or your key people from your everyday business needs for days or even hours on end. Rapid progress can be made in short bursts of activity completing the building blocks – or "gaps" – that you have already identified from the analysis and planning/deadline steps. Engage your team and give them specific items to be completed relating to their own activities and, equally as importantly as we have just discussed, their interaction with their colleagues – or "internal customers" – who are dealing with business needs before and after their own inputs. There is nothing to stop you bringing key suppliers and subcontractors into the process. They will be affected so encourage their cooperation; you just never know where some real gold will come from.

Always remember that at audit time the Auditor will be obliged to assess whether "you do what you say you do". The processes that you describe in your manual will be "live tested"; the Auditor, who is under scrutiny himself, will be looking for objective evidence of your described processes. So keep them simple, over-sophistication is your enemy both at audit time and when trying to fully implement your System. Satisfy more than one ISO Requirement whenever and wherever you can.

All Requirements of the Standards to which your Integrated Management System purports to satisfy must be addressed within your manual. Only then will you be ready to undergo a Stage 1 Audit.

Step 6: Stage 1 Audit

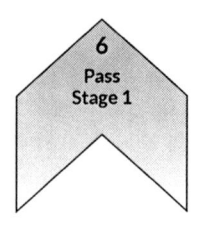

Remember that the Stage 1 Audit is a Document Review. An Auditor will visit you and conduct a desk based audit on your Integrated Management System manual (and any other supporting documentation that you refer to within it). This is where the manual you have built in the Construction step is put under scrutiny.

Your consultant's job is to make sure that your manual is compliant in every respect. Throughout the Construction step he or she must ensure that every Requirement of the Standards has been satisfied by your business in an

Chapter 14 – The 8 Step Methodology

appropriate manner. You need to work with him to ensure that your solutions are practical and achievable consistently. Can you do what you say you do?

No stone can be left unturned here. It is always my intention to make the Auditor's job simple; a clear demonstration that the Requirements of the Standards have been addressed in their entirety and applied logically and appropriately (there is no escaping that word) to the business at hand.

The Auditor must be respected. He has his job to do and there must no expectation of any concessions from him. Why would you? You want a robust audit that seriously assesses the Integrated Management System manual that you have addressed. While it obviously must be compiled for your business needs it is sensible to present a document that logically addresses the Requirements in a recognisable format.

There is no need to get hung up about passing the audit without any issues whatsoever. No consultant worth his salt would ever let you go forward with even a remote hint of a major non-conformance but a few minor non-conformances are not the end of the world. Should they occur they are clearly an opportunity for improvement. While an Auditor is not allowed to offer consultancy advice he could well have very valuable comments contained within his non-conformity reporting. Any non-conformances clearly must be addressed and closed out before the Stage 2 Audit.

Part of the reason **for** a Stage 1 Audit is to have this initial assessment, to receive the Auditor's feedback and also of course to have the opportunity and time to make any necessary adjustments and improvements before Stage 2 Audit. It is very common indeed that manuals change between stages 1 and 2. And why not, is that not ISO in action? Improvement!

Chapter 14 – The 8 Step Methodology

Step 7: Stage 2 Audit

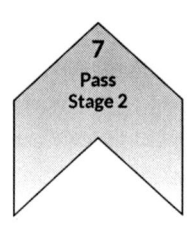

In between audits at Stage 1 and Stage 2 there are certain activities that must take place and it is quite legitimate that these are done between stages rather than done before Stage 1 Audit. Moreover, feedback from Stage 1 can inform the activities that you must undertake.

By the time a business gets to this stage I usually find that creative momentum is in full flow, especially if quite a few people have been involved. The Integrated Management System manual is now a live document, it is tangible and people want it to be right. When the Stage 1 Audit feedback is added to the mix it is not unusual to see the manual go through quite a bit of change before the Stage 2 Audit. And of course as processes are tested by the business in the field, and are therefore coming up against more staff who are charged with operating them, then recommendations for improvement start to fly around. This is to be encouraged and celebrated. As I said above, this is ISO in action.

The Requirements that must be fulfilled between stages add more grist to this particular mill. Internal Audit is the first one. There is nothing to stop you carrying out Internal Audits before a Stage 1 Audit, but I think between stages is the right time. You will have had your System reviewed and approved for continuance to Stage 1 Audit by your consultant and you will have had feedback from the Auditor at the document review. Now you should test your System yourself, via Internal Audit, before your independent live test of your System at Stage 2 Audit. I will talk about Internal Audits in more detail in the next chapter. Before Stage 2 Audit however, you need to compile a programme for Internal Audits covering the whole of your System.

The second activity/requirement is to conduct a Management Review and the results and feedback from Internal Audits must form an agenda item for that meeting. The Management Review of course goes well beyond looking at Internal Audits. Again I feel the timing is right. The manual has been built, staff will have been testing it, a Stage 1 Audit has taken place and Internal Audits have been conducted. It is time for Top Management to convene a meeting to assess the suitability and effectiveness of the Integrated Management System manual that has been created. Is it what you want? Does it serve your business? It is quite likely that this review will trigger even more changes to your system before Stage 2 Audit.

A major output of the Management Review is the setting of improvement Objectives and Targets with a programme, means of achieving and responsibility for their achievement. You will have plenty of objectives by this time. They will be coming at you from your staff's experience of the new System, from the Stage 1, from the Internal Audits and from the Management Review. You are now ready for the Stage 2 Audit and the Auditor will certainly look at your Internal Audits, your Management Review minutes, and your Objectives programme. The absence of, or incorrect attempt at, just anyone of them will seriously jeopardise your chances of Stage 2 success.

Step 8: Continual Improvement

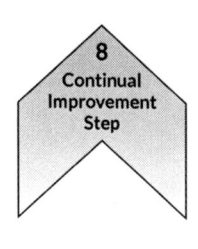

Successful ISO Certification, especially for an Integrated Management System, is a major achievement and is to be celebrated. You really should be shouting from the rooftops. Get the UKAS logos and add them to your company literature; emblazon your success all across your website; tell your customers and your supply chain. Tell potential customers as well!

In many ways however Certification is just the end of the beginning.

Chapter 14 — The 8 Step Methodology

You have certainly made a massive statement to your customers, your suppliers and your wider community. Your business will certainly be easier and less stressful to control. You will have opened doors to new markets and customers previously excluded from you. The real value however lies in the months and years ahead as your System evolves and you improve year on year. You have the tools to do so and we will look at how they improve your business in the last chapter.

Summary

The eight steps to guaranteed ISO success:

- Step 1: Preliminary
- Step 2: Visualisation
- Step 3: Analysis
- Step 4: Planning and Deadline
- Step 5: Construction
- Step 6: Stage 1 Audit
- Step 7: Stage 2 Audit
- Step 8: Continual Improvement

15

It's The Improvement, STUPID!

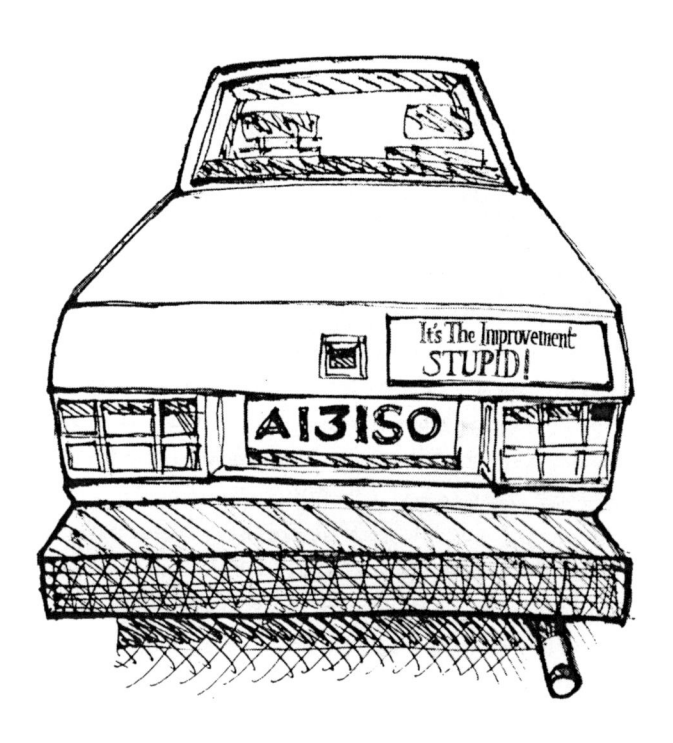

Chapter 15 — It's The Improvement, STUPID!

Throughout this book I have said that improving your business year on year is the real long-term value of developing an ISO-compliant System. Continual Improvement and customer satisfaction are the very essence of Quality Management, the former enhancing the latter, and the latter inspiring the former. It is worth recapping on some of the improvements ISO **expects** you to make. You are required to ensure that you continually improve the degree to which your products and services meet customer requirements; to continually improve the effectiveness of your processes which can only lead to improved results; and to continually improve customer satisfaction. Could there be a better blueprint for an ongoing successful business?

What would **your** business look like if it continually improved? What would your customers think of you? Your staff? What would it be like to work there?

Does your business need to improve? Most do, by their own admission, and if you are suffering from any level of quality or associated problems do you know what that is really costing you? Most poor quality issues are hidden and are dealt with, or swept under the carpet, under the radar. In these days of squeezed margins you really cannot afford financial own-goals. Failure to deliver your product or service right first time, materials wastage, inefficient use of time all erode the bottom line. A failure at the coalface can obviously have even more serious ramifications. At the very least you want your Integrated Management System to reduce such inefficiencies and have a positive financial impact. There is no reason why this cannot happen. I believe it was IBM who first used the term "poor-quality cost" and their findings were scary then and have been corroborated since. You may spend a pound in actions to prevent a quality problem from occurring in the first place; you are likely to need to spend ten times that to put a problem right once it has occurred. If the problem reaches the customer the cost of putting that right could well be a hundred times what it would have cost to prevent it in the first instance.

Chapter 15 — It's The Improvement, STUPID!

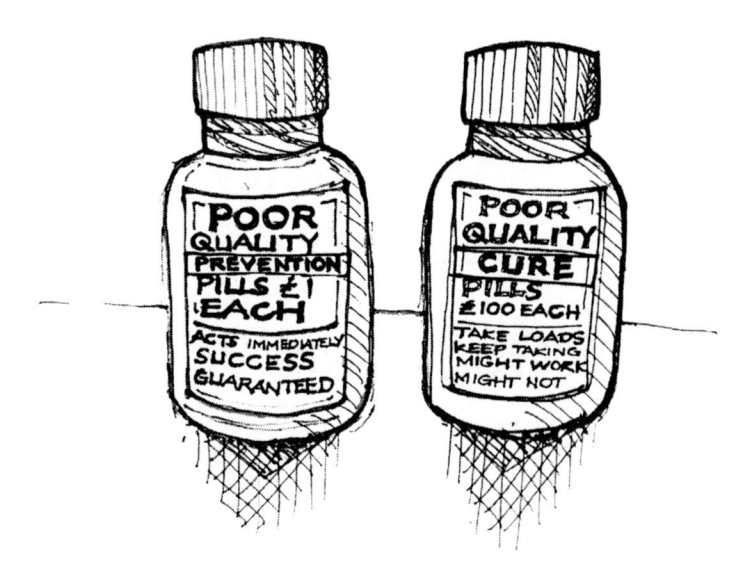

I don't think I've heard a more convincing argument for preventive action and I'll talk more about that later. The point I'm making here is that poor quality could be costing you a fortune. Even if you are still not convinced about the wisdom of developing an Integrated Management System then at least investigate how much poor quality is costing you and start putting it right. Various gurus have tried to come up with the true costs of poor quality and their ministrations have resulted in estimates of anywhere from 15% to 40% of sales. That latter figure is too shocking to contemplate so let's be conservative and say that poor quality could be costing you just 5% of sales. Your £1M turnover business could be bearing a cost of £50K per annum due to poor quality. A grand a week? In this climate? "It is always cheaper to do the job right the first time" — everyone can see the logic in that.

Chapter 15 — It's The Improvement, STUPID!

Poor quality costs money,

Good quality saves money

Is "continual improvement" possible? Is it feasible? Are there areas of your business that could be improved? Do you have a systematic process for doing so? Continual improvement starts with an attitude, a mind-set, that improvement is not only possible and desirable but also essential. You never standstill, you are either going forwards or backwards. Improvement is always possible; that is the mind-set that you have to adopt. To actually improve you need the ability and the tools to uncover the causes of problems so that you can improve systematically. You must be able to measure your improvements, indeed your performance in the first place, and you must know what has to be improved and in what sequence.

We have talked about the process approach that ISO encapsulates as being Plan-Do-Check & Act. Is that not a systematic continual improvement methodology?

Chapter 15 — It's The Improvement, STUPID!

Plan-Do-Check & Act and Continual Improvement

ISO also demands that you perform some activities aimed purely at improvement, the most obvious one being the requirement to set improvement Objectives. Such objectives often come from other activities which may initially appear to have a different focus but are in essence improvement activities:

Internal Audit is wrongly perceived sometimes as some form of policing activity but I always define internal audit as an assessment of effectiveness motivated by the desire to seek out ways of being more effective; i.e. ways of improving.

Not Just a Tick in a Box   151

Chapter 15 — It's The Improvement, STUPID!

Management Review serves many functions of immense value but in essence are we not assessing the continuing suitability and again effectiveness of our System in order to make recommendations for improvement? We will look at setting objectives, internal auditing and Management Review in detail later on but first let us return to some basics.

Developing your Integrated Management System is about defining (Plan), implementing (Do), measuring (Check) and improving (Act) your operations. Everything you do is a process that can be improved. Continual improvement springs from this Plan-Do-Check & Act model.

When planning any process initially it is easiest just to document in some way what you currently do, especially if it is working well. The sheer act of thinking about and documenting it however may lead you to seeing some immediate improvement. Performing the activity, doing it, is the real test of its effectiveness. Being tested in the field will expose any flaws, which are of course opportunities for improvement. Monitoring and measuring, checking, your process and its results will provide invaluable data on how it is performing for you. Clearly if results are not what you want then you must act to put it right, and improve it.

The specific improvement activities that ISO demands are extensions of this basic philosophy. Objectives initially arise out of the Plan phase. Management Review arises from the Do, i.e. a review of how "Do" is performing, including a review of course of the efforts to achieve Objectives! Review and analysis of data also arise from the Do phase, the data being that which you want to collect in order to provide the relevant information on how you are doing (A Factual Approach to Decision-Making!). Internal audit is clearly a Check activity. New objectives may and probably will arise from Management Review and Internal Auditing so that, as in any effective process, the circle continues. Throughout the process if anything isn't right you must Act to improve it.

Chapter 15 — It's The Improvement, STUPID!

Let us look further at the specific improvement activities of Internal Audit, Management Review and Objectives and understand how you can make these activities effective in improving your business.

Internal auditing

Internal Auditing has to be done to secure ISO Certification. Furthermore, as we know, a documented procedure for internal auditing is one of the Six Mandatory Procedures of ISO 9001. What to do when things go wrong (or "dealing with non-conformity") and Corrective Action and Preventive Action are a further three of those six Mandatory Documented Procedures. Of course these three don't spring exclusively from Internal Audit but they are so intrinsically linked as to provide more than enough fanfare to trumpet the importance of internal auditing.

A quick word about who should do Internal Audits. I believe the best people to audit an Integrated Management System are the people who built it i.e. you and your staff. Now this does immediately beg the question about competence (a fundamental ISO Principle) and you may need to consider some Internal Auditor training to satisfy these requirements. Your consultant could train you of course, and if you put an Internal Audit template together with him or her, as I do with my customers, then this should suffice. I cannot guarantee that of course, but I have never had any issues with Auditors by adopting this approach; they have been more concerned with the depth, breadth and effectiveness of the audit itself. There are also some simple but obvious rules around who should Audit what, for example an Estimator should not audit estimating, but these are easily adhered to.

When doing Internal Audits you are of course checking that your arrangements are being followed. When you have put plenty of effort into your best practice arrangements you do of course want to gauge compliance. More importantly

Chapter 15 — It's The Improvement, STUPID!

you are trying to gauge the effectiveness of your arrangements. Don't audit for the sake of it because it is a Requirement and never see Internal Auditing as an end in itself. I have seen people tense up and metaphorically hold their cards to their chest when you approach them as an internal auditor. When I tell them that together we are trying to assess if things are working around here and to see if they could be improved people lighten up. I am not auditing them as people I am auditing the process and procedures that have been wrapped around them to allow them to do their jobs in order to see if it they are effective and to see if they can be improved. Just as importantly I am asking the very people charged with executing the procedures if they can be improved. When asked to do some internal auditing for a customer recently, I attended site and was immediately met with some suspicion by the site manager who had assumed I was there to catch him out. Nothing could have been further from the truth. When I didn't pull out the dreaded "checklist" and didn't start by going through his site file his mood started to change. When I just started a conversation and asked him how he was finding things, how the office was supporting him, and how easy his job was made by their new Integrated Management System he opened up completely. We had a very productive chat and lo and behold he had some great suggestions for, yes, improvements. Now of course there were things that had to be checked in the conventional sense, especially around health & safety, and environmental issues as the company was contractually bound to do certain things. And the business had as a whole decided that certain reports were expected from the site to the office. But they were details; admittedly important details and some issues arose that had to be put right. The main point was that with a focus on what was effective for the site manager in terms of giving him the wherewithal to do his job properly a very productive "audit" ensued.

Instead of asking are you doing such and such, ask why are you doing it, and what would happen if you did it differently. When you are speaking to the people at the coalface ask them how they would like things to be improved. What irritates them? Are they being listened to?

Chapter 15 — It's The Improvement, STUPID!

The whole of your Integrated Management System needs to be audited at least once a year. You should however audit according to the importance of certain activities and the issues you face as a business. Auditing your training records for example may well be no more frequent than annually. Auditing your site performance however, your core product, will benefit from more frequent audits especially when the motivation is to gauge effectiveness rather than a simple procedural audit.

An old boss of mine used to always say, "Andrew, ask the questions that hurt!" I urge you to do the same in your Internal Audits. Questions that hurt will challenge you more than checklists to test if a certain procedure is being followed. There is obviously a role for checklists in certain circumstances but questions that hurt will drive real improvement into your business.

Just a few examples

In an internal audit, ask your staff if they see evidence of you and your Top Management colleagues demonstrating a commitment to continual improvement. Ouch! But why not ask that? You are supposed to show commitment to continual improvement and imagine the reaction you would get if you did.

Further, ask your staff if they are aware of your Quality, Environmental and Health & Safety Policies and your improvement Objectives in these areas? This may seem obvious and you might say well of course they would be, after all they are specific ISO Requirements and you would make sure that they are aware. An external Auditor is perfectly entitled to ask any of your staff whether or not they are aware of these things. Are your people aware? What if they are not? How could they contribute to your objectives if they do not know what they are? Focuses the mind a bit doesn't it!

An effective Internal Audit of this area would be able to gauge if your Quality Policy is communicated and understood and if your staff understand how they

Chapter 15 — It's The Improvement, STUPID!

contribute to achieving your objectives – they must understand and be able to explain the part they play in the achievement of your improvement objectives if they are not simply going to feel as they have a limited role around a few everyday tasks. Does your organisation have the ability to communicate this well and make people feel part of the grand plan?

When Internal Auditing your estimating and tendering arrangements ask how do you accurately determine exactly what your customers want? Does your customer always know what he wants; if he doesn't, do your estimating and tendering staff know how to fill the gaps? Pretty crucial stuff this so ask a question that hurts in order to seek out improvement.

A common area for potential problems that I see time and time again when visiting construction specialists is at the interface between various functions such as when a successful tender moves out of estimating and into the production, into the contracts department. This is a very common problem area with sometimes inadequate and/or incomplete information being passed over to the contracts team leading to any number of problems further down the line. If this is a problem for you then internal auditing of this area, asking questions that hurt, and then properly following up with effective corrective action should issues arise will undoubtedly improve it.

Another vital area, does everyone know what to do when things go wrong? Especially in relation to your product on site? Serious stuff this! Reputation at stake, contractual pressures, programme to be adhered to. How well can your business react? How do you capture the lessons learned, and does your corrective action get to the root cause and prevent it happening again? You need to know this don't you. What a business you would have if all this was in place.

Your people should know your corrective action procedure, especially as this is a Mandatory Documented Procedure. The improvement potential of

Chapter 15 — It's The Improvement, STUPID!

a properly understood and executed corrective action procedure is obvious. Killing problems off so that they do not recur is a massive step forward. Preventive action also requires a Mandatory Documented Procedure but often this proves tricky to resolve and instil into your System. Preventive action is also often not recognised as an improvement procedure in itself. As a contractor my colleagues and myself solved this one by adding a risk analysis section to our contract handover procedure (for a long time this was a problem for us, just as I have said I see it is a common problem amongst contractors now). We had developed what in time proved to be a very effective handover and added a preventive action activity at the end. We looked ahead to the forthcoming project and asked what could go wrong under a number of headings such as procurement, programme, quality demands, the particular customer, the customer's Site Manager, the particular contract. These proved to be very worthwhile conversations and led us to tailor our approach accordingly. Preventive action in action, if you see what I mean, which led to an improvement in our performance on the project in hand.

Management review

Management Review is another major tool in the improvement arsenal. As the MD/Owner you should lead this review of what your organisation came up with in the Plan phase of developing your System and indeed how it performed in the Do phase. Incidentally, Management Review is a must-do not only for the effectiveness of your whole System but also to retain your Certification, it simply cannot be omitted in any twelve month period and I would suggest you do it at least every six months to get better and better at it. Often Management Review is the first place an Auditor will start at during audits subsequent to your successful Certification. Your Management Review minutes will give him all sorts of audit trails.

It is good practice to strictly follow a comprehensive agenda for your Reviews. Are your policies still appropriate? Have the various elements of your

Chapter 15 — It's The Improvement, STUPID!

Integrated Management System performed adequately – Quality Management, Environmental Management, Health & Safety Management? What changes have occurred that could affect your System – new customers, new products, new personnel, new legislation, new environmental aspects, and new health & safety risks? Your System has to keep pace with your evolving company and Management Review is the main mechanism for doing so. You will look at the results of your Internal Audits. What did you find? What were the answers to those questions that hurt? How did your corrective action procedures perform? You will assess the contribution of your key suppliers and subcontractors and determine if their performance has been good enough for you; they are often pivotal to your delivered product and they have to be assessed and they have to develop with you. You will look at the attainment so far of the improvement Objectives that came out of the Plan phase. Are they still relevant? Have any been achieved? Have any fallen behind? Some may have been rendered obsolete by events. Are new Objectives required? Crucially, are customers getting satisfaction? Do they want more from us; can we give them more? What lessons have we learned? Can those lessons be applied to different areas of the business from which they were gleaned, thereby providing another example of preventive action **in action.** Clearly, Management Review represents so many opportunities for improvement. In fact ISO expects you to generate **recommendations** for improvement that you will take from your meeting and put them into place.

At the very least you will come out of Management Review with a revamped and updated set of Objectives, with their programmes and allocated responsibility.

Improvement objectives

Improvement Objectives are crucial – the clue is in the title. You may have had the courage to declare an ambitious Quality Policy statement and it is the selection of well-chosen targeted objectives that turn that intention into reality

Chapter 15 — It's The Improvement, STUPID!

and strive to back up the statements that you have made. They must deliver worthwhile and relevant results.

They will change inevitably and at times seem like a moving target but as long as they keep you moving forward then that is fine. No Auditor will sanction you for objectives not achieved because circumstances changed as long as your objectives have been refreshed accordingly. There will however be the ultimate sanction for their being no objectives to work to – you will fail your audit. Setting improvement objectives is the easiest way there is to demonstrate commitment to continual improvement as long as they are not just a lifeless list on a document nobody pays any attention to. What are those improvements that you always wanted to make but have been prevented from doing so by being in the trenches so long? Develop an Integrated Management System and get those "wished-for" improvements declared to your organisation – with a deadline - and provide the resources and responsibility to make sure they happen. If an objective has a deadline and somebody's name on it, it is astonishing what can be achieved. Of course, the objective must be clear and unambiguously communicated, especially in relation to desired results and how they will be measured. You must provide the means for each objective to be achieved in terms and time and resources.

As we have just seen, reviewing the status of objectives will be an agenda item at Management Review. Did they succeed and what conclusions can be drawn and lessons learned whether they did or not? Were they attempted or implemented as foreseen? Were resources provided adequate? Are the results what we wanted and do they indeed constitute the improvement we were looking for? How are customers impacted?

Chapter 15 — It's The Improvement, STUPID!

So I ask you again, what would your business look like if it continually improved? An Integrated Management System certifiable to ISO 9001, ISO 14001 and OHSAS 18001 **will** improve your business, and if implemented effectively will continually improve your business.

Summary

The Continual Improvement Tools:

- Policy Statements
- Internal Auditing
- Corrective Action
- Preventive Action
- Management Review
- Improvement Objectives

Testimonials

I was told by a large customer that I needed to have ISO 17025 to continue working with them. Andrew Foy was recommended to me by a Contractor who had just achieved 9001/14001/18001 with Andrew's help. Andrew devised a very lean response to ISO 17025 which was vital for me as a small business. We passed the UKAS audit first time and were complemented by them on our very practical management system."

Colin Jones, Owner Aqua Plus Ltd

"Andrew has just steered my company through the process of gaining accreditation to ISO 9001, ISO 14001 and OHSAS 18001. His experience is drawn from working within the Specialist Contracting sector and having been through the same processes himself. His advice is excellent, easy to understand and implement but very relevant and I would thoroughly endorse Foy Certification Ltd. Without his gentle cajoling and expert help we would not have achieved the triple certification."

Rik Lenney, MD, Astec Projects Ltd

Chapter 15 — It's The Improvement, STUPID!

"We recently retained the services of Foy Certification to assist us in attaining our ISO certificates. I can wholly recommend Andrew and his in depth knowledge of the process and he worked above and beyond the call of duty in helping us! Thanks so much Andrew."

Paul Bagley, MD, PB Drylining Ltd

"Andrew helped us develop an Integrated Management System and obtain certification for the system under ISO9001, 14001 & 18001. Thanks to his input we achieved this in less than 12 weeks. He was able to de-mystify the process and showed us how to apply the ISO standards to develop our own existing systems. We'd recommend Andrew unreservedly to anyone considering seeking certification for these ISO standards."

Patrick Devlin, MD, Vosseler UK

We initially wanted to add ISO 14001(Environmental Management) to our existing 9001 (Quality Management) Certification. Andrew encouraged us to develop an Integrated Management System (IMS) incorporating 9001, 14001 and OHSAS 18001 (H&S Management) and we set to work. We are delighted to have just received Triple Certification for our IMS; the first in our sector to do so and we have asked Andrew to stay on with us for a while in order to maximise the benefits.

Manny Patel, MD, Structura UK

"When I first took on the task of attempting to gain 9001, 14001 and 18001 all at once, I did not imagine the amount of work I was letting myself in for. And then along came Andrew Foy who steered me professionally with a calming influence to successfully achieve all three within 4 months. Many thanks Andrew."

Alan R J Williams. Managing Director, Farr Engineering Services Ltd

"Andrew provided a first class service, guiding us through the process and made the journey as simple and pain free as possible."

Howard Winter, MD, Sound Interiors

Testimonials

"We found Andrew to be very professional and focused on client needs to bring our company to ISO9001, 18001 & 14001 in such a short timeframe. We would recommend his services to any company."

Philip O'Reilly, Managing Director, Ridge Interiors Ltd

"Andrew has worked with our business in the past as Operations Director and subsequently providing consultation services renewing our certifications which he himself set up. We have no hesitation in recommending Foy Certification as to date they have achieved a 100% success rate."

Jim Nania, MD, Stortford Interiors

"Andrew guided us through our accreditation for ISO9001, IOS14001 & OHSAS18001. I can highly recommend Andrew to all companies considering accreditation."

Jeff Halls, MD, 20SIXLTD

"Foy Certification took the mystery out of the whole certification process. We rapidly developed an Integrated Management System conforming to the requirements of 9001/14001 and 18001 and brought control to all our activities. Pace would highly recommend Foy certification."

Mike Lidbury, Commercial Manager, Pace Contracts

"We are a young Company who had the chance of sub-contracting to some major contractors because of previous strong relationships. But we had to achieve ISO 9001, ISO 14001 and OHSAS 18001 to be part of the supply chain. Andrew convinced us that we could get there and we did! To be honest he made it logical and understandable and even enjoyable. Not only has this assured our customers but it has given us a solid foundation for future growth".

Dave Bourke, Owner Peramenter Developments

What To Do Next

I would be delighted to hear from you and help in any way I can. I would also be grateful for any thoughts on this book and how it might be improved.

Call me on 07528-571357 or email me on andrew@foycertification.com

Please visit my website to discover more about Foy Certification: www.foycertification.com

There are free downloads at www.foycertification.com/downloads/

You can also download a simple brochure at www.foycertification.com/downloads/brochure.pdf which gives just some of the pathways available to securing the Certifications your business needs.

A short conversation and maybe an email or two would allow me to give you an accurate assessment of where your business is in relation to ISO.

Good Luck.

Lightning Source UK Ltd.
Milton Keynes UK
UKOW04f0232230813

215809UK00004B/17/P

9 780957 656208